An Unexpected Journal

Superheroes

Summer 2021

Volume 4, Issue 2

Contents

SUPERHERO MOVIES ARE WORSHIP, NOT THEME PARKS

Joseph Holmes on the Attraction of Superhero Movies

Superheroes dominate our current entertainment culture. I don't think anyone would dispute that. Every year superhero films and TV shows are among the highest-grossing, highest rated, and most talked about films Hollywood releases. And this trend shows no sign of slowing down. This year alone at the movies we're getting *Black Widow*, *Shang-Chi*, *The Eternals*, *The Suicide Squad*, and *Spider-Man: No Way Home* — all of which are expected to be some of the biggest players at the domestic and global box office — after 2019's *Avengers: Endgame* broke the record to be the highest-grossing movie of all time. TV is even more saturated, with the CW giving us new seasons of *Flash* and *Supergirl* on top of the new *Superman and Lois* show, Disney+ giving us *WandaVision, Falcon and The Winter*

Soldier (both of which were some of the most talked about shows on Twitter during their runs), *Loki*, and *Miss Marvel*, Amazon's *The Boys* and *Invincible*, HBO Max's *Harley Quinn* and *Doom Patrol*, and Netflix's *Umbrella Academy* and *Jupiter's Legacy.*

This explosion of popularity in superheroes has led to something of a backlash and bewilderment on behalf of many in the film industry. Legendary film director Martin Scorsese famously wrote that superhero movies were "not cinema."

Scorsese explained, "Honestly, the closest I can think of them, as well made as they are, with actors doing the best they can under the circumstances, is theme parks. It isn't the cinema of human beings trying to convey emotional, psychological experiences to another human being."[1]

Equally legendary filmmaker Francis Ford Coppola went further. "When Martin Scorsese says that the Marvel pictures are not cinema, he's

---

[1] Catherine Shoard, "Martin Scorsese Says Marvel Movies Are 'Not Cinema'," *The Guardian*, last modified October 4, 2019, accessed May 10, 2021, www.theguardian.com/film/2019/oct/04/martin-scorsese-says-marvel-movies-are-not-cinema.

right because we expect to learn something from cinema, we expect to gain something, some enlightenment, some knowledge, some inspiration . . . I don't know that anyone gets anything out of seeing the same movie over and over again," the 80-year-old filmmaker said, according to Yahoo! News. "Martin was kind when he said it's not cinema. He didn't say it's despicable, which I just say it is."[2]

Actress and director Jodie Foster added her voice to the condemnation of superhero movies, saying, "Studios making bad content in order to appeal to the masses and shareholders is like fracking — you get the best return right now but you wreck the earth." Then, in a final jab, she said, "It's ruining the viewing habits of the American population and then ultimately the rest of the world."[3]

---

[2] Ryan Lattanzio, "Francis Ford Coppola Says Marvel Movies Are 'Despicable'," *IndieWire*, last modified October 20, 2019, accessed May 10, 2021, www.indiewire.com/2019/10/francis-ford-coppola-marvel-1202183238/.

[3] Dino-Ray Ramos, "Jodie Foster Slams Superhero Movies, Compares Studios' 'Bad Content' To Fracking," *Deadline*, last modified January 3, 2018, accessed May 10, 2021, deadline.com/2018/01/jodie-foster-black-mirror-superhero-movies-marvel-studios-dc-1202234126/.

These critics of superhero movies wrongly assume that the appeal of superhero movies is shallow and that the popularity of superheroes are both a sign and an encouragement of shallow tastes in the audience. However, this could not be further from the truth.

The reason superheroes are dominant in pop culture is because they appeal better than any other content right now in our modern society to our deep human need to worship. Far from being a shallow need which our desire to fill something bad about us, worship is a deep need that speaks to how we were created to be.

Worship and the Movies

Merriam Webster defines worship as:

(verb) 1: to honor or show reverence for as a divine being or supernatural power, 2: to regard with great or extravagant respect, honor, or devotion (a celebrity worshipped by her fans) (intransitive verb) : to perform or take part in worship or an act of worship;

(noun) 1: reverence offered a divine being or supernatural power

also : an act of expressing such reverence, 2: a form of religious practice with its creed and ritual, 3: extravagant respect or admiration for or devotion to an object of esteem, 4 (chiefly British) : a person of importance — used as a title for various officials (such as magistrates and some mayors)[4]

Taken together, these definitions match the common understanding of worship (at least in religious circles) as a universal human impulse toward extreme devotion and extravagant admiration for someone or something that inspires praise and sacrifice — whether it's toward a deity or something else. Philosopher James K.A. Smith wrote in *Desiring the Kingdom* that people are built primarily to love, and what you love most and build your life around is what you "worship."

> This sort of ultimate love could also be described as that to which we ultimately pledge allegiance; or, to evoke language that is both religious and acting, our ultimate love is what we worship.... It's not what I think that shapes my life from the bottom up; it's what I desire, what I love, that animates my passion. To be human is to be the kind of creature who is oriented

---

[4] "Worship," *Merriam-Webster*, accessed May 10, 2021, www.merriam-webster.com/dictionary/worship.

by this kind of primal, ultimate love -- even
if we never really reflect on it.[5]

People get joy from praising what they
worship. C.S. Lewis, author of *The Chronicles of
Narnia*, explains it this way in his *Reflections on
the Psalms*:

> But the most obvious fact about praise —
> whether of God or any thing — strangely
> escaped me. I thought of it in terms of
> compliment, approval, or the giving of
> honor. I had never noticed that all
> enjoyment spontaneously overflows into
> praise unless (sometimes even if) shyness
> or the fear of boring others is deliberately
> brought in to check it. The world rings with
> praise — lovers praising their mistresses,
> readers their favorite poet, walkers
> praising the countryside, players praising
> their favorite game — praise of weather,
> wines, dishes, actors, motors, horses,
> colleges, countries, historical personages,
> children, flowers, mountains, rare stamps,
> rare beetles, even sometimes politicians or
> scholars. I had not noticed how the
> humblest, and at the same time most
> balanced and capacious, minds, praised

---

[5] James K.A., Smith, *Desiring the Kingdom: Worship, Worldview, and Cultural Formation* (Ada, MI: Baker Academic, 2011), 51.

most, while the cranks, misfits and malcontents praised least . . .

I think we delight to praise what we enjoy because the praise not merely expresses but completes the enjoyment; it is its appointed consummation. It is not out of compliment that lovers keep on telling one another how beautiful they are; the delight is incomplete till it is expressed.[6]

If worship is one of the deepest parts of what it means to be human, it shouldn't surprise anyone to suggest that people go to movies in order to worship. And the data bears that out. All of the most popular and highest-grossing movies are about admirable people we want to cheer for being willing to sacrifice and die for higher ideals. Read any top box office list, including the top movies of all time.[7] You will find it populated entirely by stories that praise individuals who live up to some ideal greater than themselves. The top

---

[6] C.S. Lewis, *Reflections on the Psalms* (New York: Houghton Mifflin Harcourt, 2020), 93, Digital Edition.

[7] "These Are the Biggest Box Office Hits of All Time," *Newsday*, last modified April 26, 2021, accessed May 10, 2021, www.newsday.com/entertainment/movies/the-biggest-box-office-hits-of-all-time-1.30503303.

movies on every list are superheroes (*Avengers, Avengers: Age of Ultron, Avengers: Infinity War, Avengers: Endgame, Black Panther, Harry Potter and the Deathly Hallows Part 2, Star Wars: The Force Awakens*), romances (*Titanic, Avatar, Frozen*), royalty (*Black Panther, Frozen*), the glory of of nature (*Jurassic World, Avatar*), and the beauty of family (*Furious 7, Toy Story 3, Frozen*). All these movies draw us to cheer for people who sacrifice their lives, their fortunes, and whatever else for some ideal, whether it's their families, true love, the environment, or for their communities. These are all movies that compel us to praise the people they tell stories about, idealized men and women who sacrifice everything to defeat evil, to find true love, to defend nature, to save their families and who — every step of the way — prompt us to cheer for them as they do. You cannot find an exception anywhere. These are not merely "entertaining" movies. Comedies are entertaining, but they're barely on the list. That's because most comedies don't primarily draw you to admire anyone or anything, but rather to laugh at them, even if it's affectionately. (This is why even the highest grossing comedy of all time — *Minions* — is all about worship; it's about a group of friends looking for a master worth devoting themselves to.) These stories inspire a desire to cheer for and praise both the people we admire and the ideal they are willing to die for — whether it's the earth, romantic love, family, a city, etc.

Writers have also remarked on the similarity between the church and the movie theaters specifically — that they are both spaces built specifically designed to inspire the impulse to worship. Betsy K. Brown wrote for *Christianity Today*:

> The architecture of the church and the cinema may vary from place to place, but whether ornate or not, the structure of the buildings promise something lovely to come. We enter doors into a large, dimly-lit room. It is a hushed, open space. We sit side-by-side. We hear music. We hear carefully-chosen words. We see a place that has been set with care, a place meant to be beautiful. This aesthetic finger points toward the story that unfolds in the space — the story of the film, the story of the liturgy. Each story is new, but it is also very old. As famous screenwriter and teacher Robert McKee says, stories in film help us discover what it means to be human by

wrapping a universal experience in a culture-specific expression.[8]

The connection between religious worship and the movie theater is also a historical one. Movies have their roots in the tradition of theater, and theater has its roots in the tradition of public religious ritual. Greek theater evolved from religious celebration of Dionysus.[9] After the Roman empire collapsed, the church revived the theater within the church walls before it became so elaborate that they moved it outside to open-air performances before finally creating buildings specifically for theater: "theaters".[10] When the technology for film was invented, people tried different uses for it, but the most popular use took the form of "filmed plays" that we experience collectively in a literal "movie theater".[11] Over the

---

[8] Betsy Brown, "The Cathedral and the Movie Theater," *Christianity Today*, last modified January 29, 2015, accessed May 10, 2021, www.christianitytoday.com/ct/2015/january-web-only/cathedral-and-movie-theater.html.

[9] "The Greeks - The Origins of Theatre - The First Actor," *PBS*, accessed May 10, 2021, www.pbs.org/empires/thegreeks/background/24a_p1.html.

[10] Oscar Gross Brockett and Franklin J. Hildy, *History of the Theatre* (London: Pearson, 2014).

[11] "The History of Movies," *Understanding Media and Culture: An Introduction to Mass Communication*, accessed May 10, 2021, saylordotorg.github.io/text_understanding-media-and-culture-an-

next several decades in film, audiences consistently validated every development movies went through that made it more and more an experience built around worship, from making movies longer and bigger with *The Birth of a Nation*, the invention of the Blockbuster in the 70s with *Jaws*, and the invention of the Mega-Blockbuster in the 90s with *Titanic*.[12] In fact, the Mega-Blockbuster was so successful that Hollywood switched to making almost exclusively Mega-Blockbusters from that point on. (This is the exact opposite of Martin Scorsese's contention that people only watch Blockbusters because those are the only movies that movie theaters will show. In fact, the reason that movie theaters mostly show these movies is because when people had the choice between the kind of movies that Martin Scorsese prefers and the Blockbuster film, they consistently and overwhelmingly chose the Blockbuster.)[13]

---

introduction-to-mass-communication/s11-01-the-history-of-movies.html.

[12] Barry Langford, *Film Genre: Hollywood and Beyond* (Edinburgh: Edinburgh University Press, 2005), 244.

[13] Jason Bailey, "How the Death of Mid-Budget Cinema Left a Generation of Iconic Filmmakers MIA," *Flavorwire*, last modified December 9, 2014, accessed May 10, 2021,

It was in this context that superheroes became the main vehicles for Hollywood because they were the most effective representations for worship in cinema when worship cinema was what Hollywood was paying for.

So what is it about superheroes in particular that make them such successful worship cinema?

Why Superheroes are Perfect Worship Cinema

Worship in church involves three things that superheroes imitate better than any other film genre: admiration, audience inclusion, and iconography.

1. Admiration

In church, the object of worship is God. People gather in church to worship God by hearing sermons, seeing images, reciting prayers, and singing songs that all exist to pull the attendant's focus to the greatness of God and why he is worthy of our love and praise: his love, his mercy, his power, his faithfulness, etc. The church architecture, songs, images, and sermons tell a

---

www.flavorwire.com/492985/how-the-death-of-mid-budget-cinema-left-a-generation-of-iconic-filmmakers-mia.

story about God's goodness and power and his choice to save us at the cost of his own life — proving his praiseworthiness which is supposed to elicit praise and worship. Even the architecture is designed to draw the eye upwards to contemplate what is above you — which is God.

Superheroes, likewise, are objects of wonder and admiration. Superheroes have traits that we admire, taken to the extreme. They are strong and powerful. They are good and admirable. They are beautiful and have sex appeal. They go on adventures and have witty banter. They are independent and have interesting personalities but also can live in community with each other and have strong bonds that we are lacking in our lives. And, of course, they can confront evil and defeat it.

Most movie protagonists have traits we admire — but superheroes can push these admirable traits to their limits. Typical action-heroes like cowboys, spies, and soldiers are strong — but not Superman or even Batman strong. James Bond is a great fighter, smooth with the ladies, and deft with his great gadgets, but, to paraphrase the famous song, anything he can do, Batman and Iron Man can do better. Sports heroes are strong, but not Hulk strong. Romantic heroes are beautiful, but superheroes are equally beautiful — and have the benefit of being powerful and heroic whereas romantic heroes are ordinary and often selfish. And horror film protagonists are constantly parodied for how unadmirable they typically are.

2. Audience Inclusion

In church worship the attendee is not left to gaze upon God at a distance without access to this greatness. That would create resentment, not worship, because we love beauty that we can possess but resent beauty we cannot possess (hence the "sour grapes" fable and expression). The story that the church tells gives several ways that those who participate in church can participate in God's glory: by accepting God as Lord we gain a relationship with him and get to enjoy access to him in the same way lovers gain access to each other; we gain access to his glory by being newly related to him as his adopted children; by imitating his loving and sacrificial life we gain — in a small way — the glory that comes from doing many of the things that make him worthy of glory. This is one reason why churches tell stories of Biblical heroes as well as the martyrs and the saints: the praising and remembering the smaller deeds by fallen humans like us shows us that we can follow in God's footsteps and be worthy of smaller but similar praise.

Superheroes also make sure that we can be like the heroes we admire by making them as much *like* us as they are *better* than us. Spider-Man has superpowers and heroic morals, but he also is just an ordinary kid, has bad luck, a lousy boss, girl troubles, makes selfish choices, struggles with guilt, and has to make rent. Tony Stark is an ordinary guy with a great invention, as is Bruce Banner; Batman just has a lot of money. Even those who are not technically human like Superman, Wonder Woman and Thor look like us and behave exactly like us except for their powers. Because these characters are just like us except with powers, that gives us the perfect union of both the desire to admire something and the desire to be like the thing we admire.

Other genres with characters as powerful as superheroes lack this level of humanity that makes us feel like we could be them. Franchises like *Godzilla* or *Transformers* have monster protagonists that do not look like us and often cannot communicate with us. Therefore they rely on additional human protagonists to give us someone to relate to while the monsters give us something to admire. Superheroes more efficiently give us both the admiration and reliability in the same protagonist.

3. Iconography

One of the chief ways that church inspires worship is with its imagery and iconography. Images can hold a hundred thousand ideas, stories, concepts, feelings within them all at once that those looking at them can experience without having to think about it. This makes them very powerful in worship where they can efficiently remind the congregation of the reasons God and those who follow him are worthy of their admiration and inspire worship before a word is said — then words can be used to add more to the worship. Within the cross or crucifix of Jesus you can recall the entire story of God's self-sacrificial love and redemption of humanity. Icons and images of saints would have particular images associated with them, like halos, lambs, or walking sticks, that represent ideas that the audience would be familiar with — and which would be instant reminders of why they are worthy of admiration.

Film is primarily a visual medium, so characters who are highly visual especially fit that medium — and boy, do superheroes deliver. Like icons, superheroes wear the ideas they represent on their bodies in the form of their highly eye-catching and symbolic costumes. This keeps the ideas they represent always in front of us even when they aren't talking about those ideas. Captain America wears a flag on his chest, and Red Skull wears a Nazi symbol; this means that without saying a word, we feel every fight between them is a fight between freedom and tyranny — which makes the impact much more powerful and makes us feel it more deeply, and which frees the filmmakers up to use the dialogue to add depth and drama to these ideas. In both *Wandavision* and *Falcon and The Winter Soldier* costume changes become ways of visually representing a character's mental state, whether it's their attempt to live an idealized life or choosing to accept a new identity. Superhero costumes are the ultimate in the literary rule of "show-don't-tell."

All genres do this but always in a milder way than superheroes. Romantic comedies have men dress in masculine outfits and women in feminine outfits so we associate them with ideas of masculinity and femininity without thinking about it. James Bond's suits and Indiana Jones's hat are memorable and iconic. But superheroes' costumes are so loud and so explicit that their power is far stronger in evoking a reaction.

This is why going to a Marvel film on opening night is so similar to going to church. When I first watched the first *Avengers* film in 2012, I was surrounded by fellow fans in a movie theater watching characters I related to. We exchanged quips and admired overcome challenges and beaten bad guys. We screamed and cheered and laughed together as one so that we made each other scream and cheer and laugh harder. I had this experience again during the final battle at the end of *Avengers: Endgame*. The art form was built around giving a communal experience of worship exactly the way a church was designed to.

WHY THE BACKLASH?

This brings us back to why there is so much backlash against superheroes by some in the filmmaking community. If worship is such a deep human impulse, why do these great filmmakers dismiss these films as a shallow and debasing art form? Why is it they don't recognize these films for what they are?

Well, there is one possible — partial — explanation. They see worship as the problem.

The filmmakers who most strongly object to superhero movies have some interesting things in common with their filmography. Martin Scorsese, Francis Ford Coppola, and Jodie Foster all tend to gravitate towards the same kinds of stories: *deconstructive stories*. They tell stories that *deconstruct* their central characters rather than build up their central characters. They generally tell stories that take a person or idea that you admire and then deconstruct them before your eyes so that you can no longer admire them.

Take your average Martin Scorsese film. A handsome and talented man who is struggling to get by meets an older man who has everything he wants, so he models himself after him and becomes part of his world, which leads him to get everything he dreams of, until he discovers that the lifestyle he thought he wanted ends up destroying him and everything he cared about.

This is true whether you're talking about *Goodfellas, Raging Bull, The Wolf of Wall Street,* and even arguably *Silence.* Francis Ford Coppola similarly tells stories that are about men falling prey to corruption and deconstructing ideals, like *The Godfather, Apocalypse Now,* and *The Conversation.* Jodie Foster is the least deconstructive of the bunch, but her protagonists are almost always broken and dysfunctional people who are objects of sympathy rather than admiration.

Contrast that with your average Marvel movie, which goes the other direction. Somebody is often unadmirable, like the irresponsible Tony Stark or Thor, and then they realize that they should be better than they are, so they change and become admirable. We end by looking up to them and being inspired by them rather than being turned away from them and being disgusted by them.

To filmmakers like Scorsese, Coppola, and Foster, it might be that deconstructive filmmaking and storytelling is more truthful about the world than worshipful storytelling and therefore more meaningful. It is not that to them deconstruction is *one* truthful way to see the world, but the *most* — or perhaps only — way to see the world. (In fact, even both of Martin Scorsese's religious films, *The Last Temptation of Christ* and *Silence*, were largely about deconstructing faith.) To them, worshipful storytelling *feels* good to us but is *not good* for us. It's candy rather than real food — it's filler, but it's not what our souls really need. One can't say for certain why this is, but it could have to do with their view of the world and of the human person. They look around the world and they see that, ultimately, everyone that they admire or they see worth admiring has disappointed them, and that that instinct to worship ends up with people blindly following evil men or evil ideas, and that wisdom and truth lead you to see that the instinct to admire or worship is misplaced.

There is, of course, sense to this. You only have to turn on the news or go on Twitter to see how many people we admire regularly fall from grace and reveal themselves to be evil men and women. And from a Christian perspective, all are sinners, and anything that we worship in our life that is not God is going to let us down and draw us further into idolatry and sin. It is why Christians have historically been frightened of theater and movies and superheroes and Dungeons and Dragons and anything else that excites a human's worship because Christians know the danger of such things.

That said, the filmmaker must understand that you cannot get rid of the problem of bad worship by getting rid of worship. People are made to worship and worship is good for us. Psychology has shown the numerous benefits of worship. Worship makes people healthier and more moral. People who spend time experiencing something bigger than them that fills them with awe — such as being at the Grand Canyon, or a beautiful church, or — become more peaceful and less stressed. They also become more humble, less selfish, more loving, and more generous to others.

From *Psychology Today*:

Recent studies exploring this complex emotion have discovered compelling connections between the experience of awe and enhanced critical and creative thinking faculties, improved health, a sense of embeddedness into collective folds and an increase in pro-social behaviours such as kindness, self-sacrifice, co-operation and resource-sharing. Awe is also one of the few emotions that can reconfigure our sense of time and immerse us in the present moment.[14]

Watching stories about heroes is especially good for us. According to Jonathan Haidt, watching someone you admire causes you to experience a state called elevation. When people experience elevation, they feel a mix of awe, reverence, and admiration for a morally beautiful act. The emotion is described as similar to calmness, warmth, and love. Haidt argues that elevation is "elicited by acts of virtue or moral beauty; it causes warm, open feelings in the chest."[15] The emotion of elevation, which warms and uplifts us, also includes a desire to become a better person. According to Haidt, elevation "motivates people to behave more virtuously themselves."[16] The elevation we feel upon

---

[14] Emma Stone, "The Emerging Science of Awe and Its Benefits," *Psychology Today*, last modified April 27, 2017, accessed May 10, 2021, www.psychologytoday.com/us/blog/understanding-awe/201704/the-emerging-science-awe-and-its-benefits.

[15] Scott T. Allison, "5 Surprising Ways That Heroes Improve Our Lives," *Psychology Today*, last modified April 16, 2014, accessed May 10, 2021, www.psychologytoday.com/us/blog/why-we-need-heroes/201404/5-surprising-ways-heroes-improve-our-lives.

[16] Ibid.

witnessing a heroic act transforms us into believing we are capable of heroic acts ourselves.

Moreover, if history has taught us anything, it is that getting rid of one object of worship doesn't stop people from worshiping, but simply causes humans to replace it with another. David Foster Wallace famously wrote that everyone worships. "There is no such thing as not worshipping. Everybody worships. The only choice we get is what to worship."[17] The Enlightenment project to get rid of God only made men replace it with fascism, communism, patriotism, materialism, individualism, and a million other secular objects of worship. There really is no way to keep people from worshiping.

So the solution cannot be to get rid of worship but to direct people to the right object of worship. In fact, you might say that filmmakers like Martin Scorsese have aided the success of superhero movies by not making movies that feature alternative objects of worship. If all you do is deconstruct, you

---

[17] Mike Knetzger, "'Everybody Worships: What Do You Worship?", David Foster Wallace, *Medium*, last modified March 12, 2020, accessed May 10, 2021, medium.com/@mike.knetzger/everybody-worships-what-do-you-worship-david-foster-wallace-52f3bcf2287f.

leave people vulnerable to anyone who has an alternative to put in its place.

Christians, likewise, often worry that superhero movies will cause people to worship superheroes rather than God. And it is true that it would be much better if people spent more time worshiping at church than they do worshiping at the movies. But like with the deconstructive filmmakers, this says more about the failure of churches to make their worship as compelling as movies are. It is a call to Christian filmmakers to make their movies that worship God as compelling as superhero movies are. Moreover, saying superhero movies cause people to worship superheroes isn't really true. Superheroes do not draw worship toward themselves, but toward their ideals. We know this because superheroes fight for others and are willing to die for things that they believe are greater than themselves — meaning that the heroes themselves are not the meaning of life but simply point the way to the meaning of life. A superhero who does not do this is simply not a superhero in the traditional sense. This is the difference between an icon and an idol. An idol draws worship toward itself, and an icon directs worship elsewhere. The only question is whether the heroes are fighting for ideals that are the right ideals or the wrong ideals.

None of this is to say that there is no place for primarily deconstructive storytelling like that preferred by Martin Scorsese and Francis Ford Coppola. And none of this is to say that the world would not be better with more variety in movies. One of the great things about Netflix is that it has created a business model that has made the mid-budget movie financially viable again. Far from crowding out weird indie films, superhero movies have elevated the profile of directors like Taka Wattiti to the degree that there is greater attention and money for their smaller indie projects.

The point is this: the reason for the popularity of superheroes today is not because of something *wrong* with us, but because of something *right* with us. We are meant to worship. Those who wish to elevate different types of stories need to learn from what the love of superheroes tells us about the human person and the deepest parts of their needs.

Worth Reading

Jason M. Smith on Some Good Starting Points

Worth Reading is An Unexpected Journal's book recommendations column. Each issue we highlight a few titles, related to that issue's theme, that are recommended by AUJ staff, contributors, or readers. Books featured here could be from any genre, for readers of any age, published at any time. What they have in common is that people who appreciate the work and goals of An Unexpected Journal believe them to be Worth Reading.

To contribute your favorite book to Worth Reading, write ~500 words explaining why it's a good book and a good fit for an upcoming issue and use the Submissions form to send it in.

*   *   *

Thanks to nearly two decades of box-office films and small-screen superhero shows, most of us are much more familiar with cinematographic reimaginings of classic twentieth-century Marvel and DC characters than we are with the comic books and graphic novels these characters came from. Yet these, and many other stories born of graphic novels, feel like they're everywhere in pop culture these days. "Catching up" is neither possible nor desirable: as with books of any medium, thousands of graphic novels probably aren't worth reading. But if, like me, you didn't grow up reading comics, but you're curious about why they're so beloved, a good entry point to the genre for well-read adults is Alan Moore's *V for Vendetta*.

V for Vendetta (the graphic novel) is cleverer and more literary than *V for Vendetta* (the film). The film's not bad as adaptations go, but the graphic novel is stunning. You're likely familiar with illustrator David Lloyd's iconic artwork (that bemusingly expressive Guy Fawkes mask) or writer Alan Moore's masterful wordplay (alliterative dialogue deploying more words beginning with the letter "v" than you remembered existed in the English lexicon). But if you haven't read the novel, you haven't had a chance to appreciate the breadth of Moore's vision or the carefully-crafted way the story unfolds.

V for Vendetta is dystopian in the tradition of Orwell and *1984*: a fascist government has taken over Great Britain in the wake of horrific germ warfare strikes by terrorists unknown. Thanks to careful information control, the public is unaware that these strikes were carried out by power-hungry domestic conspirators within the English government and that the weaponized bacterial agent was developed by their own military by experimenting on so-called "undesirables." By creating and leveraging widespread fear, the conspirators were able to put themselves on top of a new, authoritarian regime -- one that the story's protagonist, the self-styled V, has taken it upon himself to topple.

Aesthetically, the story has a retro-futuristic sci-fi feel. Like the original *Star Trek* TV show, Moore's story was imagined well before computers were portable or the internet existed, but is set in an alt-history timeline projected forward -- in this case, to the 1990s. Political thriller, espionage tales, even a bit of film noir are evident influences, as are the actual headlines of twentieth-century horrors, tragedies, scandals, and challenges. Moore brings all of these together to create a grippingly plausible scenario of authoritarian evil. Even those living in the world's freest nations will be driven to ponder the steps of transformation between our governments and V's; the number of those steps can be frighteningly few, and seeing them may just inspire readers toward more proactive citizenship. Unless democracy is vigilantly preserved by its own people, Moore seems to warn, rescuing an oppressed and fearful populace could be left up to someone destructive like V: no savior, but rather a heroic incarnation of poetic justice. (Elaborating on this point would be spoilers, but let's just say that *V for Vendetta*'s would-be autocrats accidentally recreated V as an incarnation of karmic retribution during their march to power). By attending carefully to real history as well as their literary predecessors, Moore and illustrator David Lloyd bring to life a story simultaneously dark, prophetic, and hopeful in *V for Vendetta*.

*   *   *

For aspiring graphic novelists, *The DC Comics Guide to Writing Comics* by industry veteran

Dennis O'Neil is the definitive work. Lots of resources exist for illustrators, but writing for visual media - especially an art form as constrained as a graphic novel - is no mean feat. (The number one mistake made by amateur comics writers? Scripting two actions into a single panel!) O'Neil introduces readers to nuts-and-bolts like the terminology used (displayed side-by-side with examples) and standard script formats, along with more subjective techniques for character development (you have very few words to work with, remember) and crafting story arcs for everything from a one-off issue to a larger series. He shows writers clearly and carefully how to imagine a story in terms of a sequence of visual panels and describe that sequence in a way that professional illustrators will be able to translate to the page of a comic book. *The DC Comics Guide to Writing Comics* is an invaluable resource for anyone who wants to, as Emily Dickinson advises, "Tell all the truth but tell it slant" in the form of graphic novels.

*   *   *

But stories of superheroes are not limited to graphic novels and comics, nor to human characters. For a superhero story like few others, find a copy of Walter Wangerin Jr.'s *The Book of the Dun Cow*. In it, Chanticleer the Rooster must rally the other farm animals, rallying and deploying each creature's unique abilities, to guard the world against the long-imprisoned Wyrm, its harbinger Cockatrice, and a mud-swollen river which threatens to drown the farm and soften Wyrm's subterranean prison, allowing the Great Enemy to break free.

Until the rise of Cockatrice and the coming of the Creator's emissary the Dun Cow, Chanticleer the Rooster did not know he had the special powers known as *crows potens*. He believed his crowing was meant merely to mark the hours and give order to the passing of night and day. What he does know is that he has a guilty secret from his past, from before he came to the farm: a supersuit, of sorts -- a pair of fighting spurs, hidden away in the straw at the top floor of the roost.

The Book of the Dun Cow starts soothingly, using familiar animal-story tropes to orient the reader (a proud rooster, a mournful hound, comedic hyperbole) but as pages turn (and the rain comes down) and stakes get higher (and the rain comes down), the power of evil grows in the distance. Information critical to the farm's survival is locked behind trauma; crucial communication is hampered by pride and awkwardness (and all the while the hellish infested river is rising). The opening pages might lead one to suspect that this is a book to read aloud to young children, but do read it yourself all the way through once before deciding. Even animal stories can get dark.

Yet Wangerin Jr. treats the foibles and flaws and ugly self-serving mistakes of his characters with surprising gentleness. Their sins are faced boldly, but neither explained away nor judged. The manner of narrative is almost priestly, in the best possible sense of the word. Even as he shapes an epic conflict between Good and Evil, Wangerin Jr. continuously reminds the reader that there is only one Enemy here, and its name is Wyrm.

Metaphysically, *The Book of the Dun Cow* is reminiscent of *Watership Down*, which, despite being a retelling of the *Aeneid* (with rabbits), is almost totally absent of gods. But in this story there is Wyrm, a hideously enfleshed yet protocosmic being; and there is God, a divine force for good, physically absent but undeniably involved. The best evidence for divine intervention in the world of the Dun Cow are the animals themselves, and the commonplace gifts for heroism they've held all along.

*   *   *

Have a book Worth Reading? Write ~500 words explaining why and send it in using the Submissions form on our website. http://anunexpectedjournal.com/submissions

Person or Persona:
What's Inside the Spider-Verse?

Cherish Nelson on Plantinga's
Conception of the Multiverse

With the explosion of serialized superhero films over the last decade, talk of a multiverse has never been more integrated into popular culture. The term 'multiverse' is a combination of the words 'multiple' and 'universe' used to describe the existence of multiple worlds or realities. While terms like 'multiverse' may occasionally be used to refer to possible universes outside our known Milky Way Galaxy, that is not the definition of the household version popularized by the Marvel Cinematic Universe.[1] Alternate possible universes is also not the definition that Alvin Plantinga uses when he discusses other possible worlds in his

---

[1] The MCU does include films with galaxies outside our own, like the *Thor* and *Guardians of the Galaxy* series. Still, these films exist within the single, original universe established by the MCU. 'Multiverse' does not refer to Thor's Asgard or to any of the planets from *Guardians of the Galaxy*.

book *God, Freedom, and Evil.* When Plantinga discusses possible worlds, he refers to worlds that could logically exist, not ones that actually exist, as in the multiverse. Spiritual implications surrounding a potential multiverse abound, but one of the most pressing is the question of what defines each of us as a unique human being. Examining Alvin Plantinga's discussion of *essence* in *God, Freedom, and Evil* alongside Sony's and Marvel's *Into the Spider-Verse* can help us recognize that a multiverse erases *essence,* which is the mark of humanity.

In *God, Freedom, and Evil,* Plantinga uses Socrates to illustrate what he means by a person's essence. Plantinga writes that we can "define Socrates' *essence* as the set of properties essential to him . . . and this set contains all his world-indexed properties, together with some others."[2] The existence of multiple Spider-People sharing essential properties across the Spider-Verse parallels Plantinga's concept of essence. The various Spider-Man characters, including a Spider-Pig and Spider-Woman, share the defining

---

[2] Alvin Plantinga, *God, Freedom, and Evil* (Grand Rapids: William B. Eerdmans Publishing Company, 1974), 51.

characteristics of the original Peter Parker Spider-Man. They all were bitten by radioactive spiders; their hero's journeys began with the deaths of loved ones; they wear spider costumes and use web-like technology; they all strive to protect their cities. They even share a personal mantra, which is revealed as the multiverse heroes work to train Miles Morales to become his world's new Spider-Man: get up after falling down.[3]

While the Spider-Man characters' shared attributes can help us imaginatively understand Plantinga's discussion of essence, a critical reading of *God, Freedom, and Evil* demands that we distinguish *essence* from what we see with the heroes of *Into the Spider-Verse*. We ought to object to calling these properties Spider-Man's essence because the sets of properties identified as the potential essence of Spider-Man are only similar, not identical. For example, Gwen Stacy becomes Spider-Woman because Peter Parker died in her world, but Peter Parker becomes Spider-Man because Uncle Ben died in his world.[4]

---

[3] *Spider-Man: Into the Spider-Verse*, directed by Bob Persichetti, Peter Ramsey, and Rodney Rothman (Sony Pictures, 2018), Amazon Prime Video.

[4] *Spider-Man, 2018.*

Death is a common factor in the making of each person's hero, but the deaths and circumstances are not identical. An important distinction is necessary, however. We must remember that when Plantinga discusses *essence*, he is referring to people. In fact, Plantinga mentions that one's essence is maximal, "a complete set of world-indexed properties." *Essence* is the whole of a person. Spider-Man's essence-like quality is defined by a general set of characteristics while a human's essence is defined by a specific set of properties. As we see in the film, there are differences in the attitudes of each hero. Therefore, Gwen Stacy, Peter Parker, and Miles Morales could have an essence, but their hero characters could not. Spider-Man is a persona, not a person. Therefore, Spider-Man does not have an essence the same way human beings have an essence.

In *Into the Spider-Verse*, the characters' shared hero-making characteristics are more like an ethos — the characteristic spirit of Spider-People that guides their ideals — than an essence. These characteristics make a distinguished character for the Spider-Man persona, but they don't create a fundamental, unwavering definition for a being. Miles Morales confirms this idea in his final monologue when he says, "Anyone can wear the mask. You could wear the mask. If you didn't know that before, I hope you do now."[5] Though Spider-Man exists in multiple worlds, that character is not tied to the essence of any particular person. This thought is intended to encourage viewers to believe in their power to be heroes, but it ignores the fundamental truth that a person's essence is what allows him or her to adopt the Spider-Man ethos. Here, Miles forgets how significantly each hero's experiences shaped him or her into the Spider-Man persona. Experiences shape the set of properties attributed to a person, which is one's essence. Without those experiences, a person cannot take on the Spider-Man persona without fundamentally altering the ethos of that persona.

Viewers can also recognize a missing *essence* when we look at characters like Peter Parker, Mary Jane, Gwen Stacy, and Miles Morales. When he discusses the idea of possible worlds, Plantinga writes, "It would be a mistake, of course, to think of all of these worlds as somehow 'going on' at the

---

[5] *Spider-Man, 2018.*

same time, with the same person reduplicated through these worlds and actually existing in a lot of different ways."[6] This concept, however, is exactly what we see in *Into the Spider-Verse*. We see two different versions of both Mary Jane and Peter Parker, which implies that Miles Morales and Gwen Stacy also both exist in at least two different worlds. There are characters from two totally different worlds that are nothing like Miles's world. There is also a talking, cartoonish Spider-Pig and a noir version of a Peter Parker Spider-Man who exists in a black-and-white world. *Into the Spider-Verse* reveals the problem of a potential multiverse: human beings have no 'self' if they exist in more than one actual world.

Because Miles, Peter, and the others are people and not personas, they will not have essences if multiple real versions exist. Peter Parker perfectly reveals this truth. His multiple versions are the only ones compared in the film. In Miles's world, Peter Parker is blonde, but Peter Parker prime has brown hair. Then we also have noir Peter Parker who is devoid of color and far less sarcastic than the other Peters. Finally, of

---

[6] Plantinga, *God, Freedom, and Evil,* 37.

course, we have Peter Porker, the pig version of Peter Parker.[7] We do not have a maximal set of properties that allow us to define Peter Parker. In fact, we have contradicting properties: different hair colors, being devoid of color, or being a pig. If we saw three versions of Peter Parker where Peter Parker prime and noir Peter Parker were merely missing some of the characteristics of Mile's version of Peter, we could look at the Spider-Verse differently. The world of Miles Morales would be the actual world, and all the other worlds would be mere possible worlds. However, that is not what we see. We see five distinct, actual worlds with unique human and humanoid characters. Because we see that Peter is distinct even from himself across at least three worlds, we cannot completely and specifically answer the question 'Who is Peter Parker?' We can only speak generally of him. Without this maximal set of properties, Peter Parker has no essence. He becomes indistinguishable from a persona, like the character Spider-Man, and loses his unique marker of humanity.

---

[7] *Spider-Man*, 2018.

What, then, exists inside the Spider-Verse? It's certainly not people. After examining *God, Freedom, and Evil* in tandem with *Into the Spider-Verse*, we can see that exploring the idea of a multiverse erases the mark of humanity in a character. Plantinga is right to call it a mistake to understand the multiverse the same way we understand possible worlds. We may enjoy the multiverse as a plot device since it provides an easy, consequence-free way to watch characters endure new trials and even come back from the dead, but we ought not accept the multiverse as possible truth if we believe that we are all uniquely marked with God-breathed souls.

GLOBAL SUPERHEROES FROM THE DISNEYVERSE AND STUDIO GHIBLI

Seth Myers on Heroism Manifested around the World

"Of course, there are universal rules to which all goodness must conform. But that's only the grammar of virtue. It's not there that the sap is. He doesn't make two blades of grass the same: how much less two saints, two nations, two angels. The whole work of healing Tellus depends on nursing that little spark, on incarnating that ghost, which is alive in every real people, and different in each. When Logres really dominates Britain, when the goddess Reason, the divine clearness, is really enthroned in France, when the order of Heaven is really followed in China, why, then it will be spring."

C.S. Lewis, *That Hideous Strength*[1]

---

[1] C.S. Lewis, *That Hideous Strength* (New York: Scribner, 2003), 369.

"He doesn't make two blades of grass the same, much less two saints, two nations." With that recognition of the spark of the divine, the imprint of God in an act of cultural *imago Dei* which is the face of God uniquely seeded in all cultures, C.S. Lewis sounds an optimistic note that resonates throughout many of the heroic, coming of age stories produced by Disney Pictures for emergent (though often long-established) cultures and Studio Ghibli. This statement by Lewis is reflected in his *Abolition of Man* treatise on the state of moral education, as he provides an appendix chronicling the universal moral code found throughout all of the world's great cultures. That he gives the code an Eastern name, the *Tao*, and cites the Indian moral code of the *Rta* as well as that of the Ancient Greeks speaks of his conviction that such sparks of a divine code can be found in all cultures. We will trace these virtues by examining various heroic Disney films set in the diverse cultures of many lands: the Latin American culture in *Coco* (2017), African-American culture in *Soul* (2020, augmented by perspectives from *Black Panther* and *Coming 2 America*), Middle Eastern culture in *Aladdin* (2019), Chinese culture in *Mulan* (2020) and the cultures of

Southeast Asia in *Raya and the Last Dragon* (2021). The list of Disney films is augmented by Hiyao Miyazaki's critically acclaimed anime *Spirited Away* (2001); a series of his Miyazaki's Studio Ghibli films have played annually in American theaters in recent years, showing their global appeal. The moral courage required of the typically young heroes in these works will be shown to reflect values found in the literature, both classic and contemporary, from their respective cultures. The lessons and values, however, are universal and amount to those of J.R.R. Tolkien's *Lord of the Rings* and the One Ring of Power: basic human values like dignity, love, and respect are at risk from those who would exploit others. Heroes, however personally flawed they might be, fight for these values which cloak humanity in its dignity; superheroes are simply heroes somehow granted special powers. Invoking the element of the fantastic in stories with heroic struggles dominates the fantasy genre (in which the world itself is a fantastic creation), and fuels the more recent literary tradition of *magical realism*. As the genre of magical realism is used in literature from around the globe, a quick survey of its history can help us empathize with issues faced by the cultures presented here.

The genre of *magical realism* (a variant of sorts of both surrealism and fantasy) was initiated in the 1920s by German art critic Franz Roh and describes highly realistic portrayals which yet hint at the magical nature of the world. It soon carried over into the literary field by predominantly Latin American authors and artists, the genre often being referred to as *lo real maravilloso* (marvelous realism) and *realism magico*. The magically real is distinguished from its cousin *surrealism*, typically a projection of the psychological, and from *fantasy*, as it uses a primarily realistic rather than fantastic world.

The genre was re-introduced by Colombian author Gabriel Marcel Marquez's 1967 novel *One Hundred Years of Solitude*, but it has influenced literature in Japan, the Middle East, and Africa among other areas, though one can even claim the pedigree for the stories of Mark Twain and Southern Renaissance/Gothic works by William Faulkner. For Marquez and others who employ such fantastic elements, the effect is to ennoble national mythologies and counter the depressing realism of modern rationality in its often capitalist and imperialist guises. As one summary states:

> Various critics have used [the term magical realism] to characterize texts of other so-called emergent cultures . . . as well as texts of migrant literature . . . [and] underscored its function as a differential mode of literary expression that valorizes a discourse whose perceptual orientation is essentially non-Western.[2]

In Japanese literature, the genre is used to critique Japanese society itself, as in its modernization efforts to emulate the West, critics claim that they suppressed their own cultural traditions.

Missiologists as well recognize that non-Western cultures are more accepting of non-rational, if not fantastic, aspects of reality. Paul Hiebert describes a "middle level of supernatural this-world beings and forces" as an "excluded middle" between the worlds of science and religion as typically understood by Westerners.

---

2 John Erickson, "Metoikoi and Magical Realism in the Maghrebian Narratives of Tahar ben Jelloun and Abdelkebir Khatibi" in *Magical Realism: Theory, History, Community*, ed. Lois Parkinson Zamora and Wendy B. Faris (Durham: Duke University Press, 1995), 427. Digital edition.

Whereas modern, rational, and scientifically sophisticated Westerners tend to see the world as lifeless matter controlled by impersonal forces, "many tribal religionists see the world as alive."[3] Leslie Newbigin, missiologist to India, argued that the Western mindset often discounted this perspective, and Christian missions became one of the greatest secularizing forces in history.[4] Superheroes (or mythical heroes, such as Aladdin or arguably Mulan), whether supported by current trends in literature, seen at the movies, or resonating with long held worldviews, are particularly helpful in understanding the hopes and fears of any culture, Western or non-Western.

As we move from West to East, we pair recent (and typically Disney) films with novels from the cultures examined, considering the role and perspective of faith for each. In this way, we can better understand Latin America (Disney's *Coco* paired with Marquez's *100 Years of Solitude*), the Middle East (Disney's *Aladdin* and various versions of *The Thousand and One Nights*), African

---

[3] Paul G. Hiebert, *Anthropological Reflections on Missiological Issues* (Grand Rapids: Baker Books, 1999), 197.

[4] Ibid.

American culture (Disney's *Soul, Black Panther,* and Paramount's *Coming 2 America,* and various African post-colonial authors), China (Disney's *Mulan* and the *Tale of the Red Chamber* from the 1800s), Southeast Asia and India (*Raya and the Last Dragon* and Salmon Rushdie's *Midnight's Children*), and finally Japan (Studio Ghibli's *Spirited Away* and the medieval *The Tale of Genji* and some contemporary works of Haruki Murakami), and better understand the values which make today's heroes.

Coco: Where the Magic and the Music All Begins

Coco, like all of the films and their heroes reviewed here, is a coming-of-age tale and features a 12-year-old boy Miguel who struggles to find his identity as a musician though his family is the only one in Mexico which hates music.[5] The story is set around the Mexican holiday of the Day of the Dead, a traditional holiday to honor ancestors. It arguably originated as the Catholic All Saints Day of remembrance and prayers for the deceased (though some claim its origins in

---

[5] *Coco,* directed by Lee Unkrich, (Walt Disney Pictures, October 2017).

ancient Aztec rituals). It has become a secular, national holiday and a symbol of common heritage in modern times. Today, it is regarded more as a day of celebration than mourning, as a quip describes it with "there is more life than time," celebrating the enduring legacy of the past.[6]

For Miguel, finding himself involves a struggle both against and for his family. His grandmother Coco was abandoned as a child by her musician father, after which her family survived as shoemakers ("music tore the family apart, but shoes brought them together"); as a result, Miguel is forbidden from pursuing the career he loves, despite aspiring to be a great guitarist like the famous Ernesto whom he deduces to be his great-great-grandfather. When Miguel takes Ernesto's famous guitar from a display after his own is destroyed by his grandmother, he gains the ability to see and communicate with his departed ancestors whom he visits in the Land of the Dead. Miguel is also cursed, however, as by stealing from the dead he loses contact with the

---

[6] Thematically enough, I found this at a Day of the Dead display at Disney's Mexico village area of their Epcot theme park in Orlando, Florida.

living; the curse can only be reversed by gaining a blessing from an ancestor. Since Miguel can receive a blessing from his great-great-grandmother only on the condition that he give up music, he instead seeks out Ernesto to prove himself and receive a blessing. Fate tricks Miguel, however, when he discovers Ernesto is not the great ancestor he seeks, but his actual great-great-grandfather's nemesis who stole both his music and his life. The story's moral of the importance of both love and sacrifice for family is wrapped neatly in Ernesto's famous song, "Remember Me," which turned out to be a song written by Miguel's actual great-great-grandfather for his baby daughter Coco. Upon learning this, Miguel finds that he is finally proud of his family.

Miguel's heroism consists of enduring various challenges to find his great-great-grandfather as well as to help him return to the land of the living to once more see Coco. Family is particularly important in Latin American culture, a reflection ultimately of how the Christian Trinity is a family into which we are invited. Anselm claimed that love is the root of the Trinity, "from the Father and the Son together, floods forth ... Love" and "Love can be called the Spirit of the Father and the Son," Paul claims we are "heirs of God, and joint-heirs with Christ," and Jesus declared that "I call you not servants, but . . . friends, for all that I have heard from the Father I have shared with you." [7] [8] [9] Aristotle's observation that "man is a political animal . . . [since] a social instinct is implanted in all men by nature" has no higher fulfilment in the family and ultimately in the divine communion which is God's family.[10]

In an optimistic Disney moment, Miguel sings his father's song with the lyrics "the world is my family, and music is my language," which evokes imagery from John Piper's *Let the Nations Be Glad!* that the divine music of worship by the nations and the redeemed is God's purpose for this world, and from Lewis who applauded the diversity of God's creation, considering that "if all experienced God in the same way and returned Him an identical worship, the song of the church

---

[7] Anselm of Canterbury, *Monologion* 54,57 in *Anselm of Canterbury: The Major Works* (Oxford: Oxford University Press, 2008), 62-64.

[8] Romans 8:17, KJV.

[9] Matthew 15:15, KJV.

[10] Aristotle, *Politics,* Book I, Ch. 2.

triumphant would have no symphony, it would be an orchestra in which all the instruments played the same note."[11] [12] The heroic, musical Miguel can teach us the importance of loyalty to and sacrifice for family, as well as the joy of music, all of which reflect a deeper meaning and glory.

Latin American literature reflects the centrality of family, as well as indigenous and foreign influences on the Latin culture. Colombian author Marquez's 1967 novel *One Hundred Years of Solitude* is a key work for understanding contemporary Latin American literature and culture. Fantastic happenings are included in his story of the mythical Latin American town of Macondo and the Buendia family. They endure the disruptions of dictatorships, corporate exploitation, and consequences of actions from previous generations while otherwise enjoying fantastic events such as rainstorms of flowers, supernatural curses and blessings, and prophecies concerning their fate. Marquez claims to have simply told such fantastic tales in the

[11] John Piper, *Let the Nations Be Glad!* (Grand Rapids: Baker Academic, 2010), 1.

[12] C.S. Lewis, "Heaven" in *The Problem of Pain* (New York: HarperOne, 2000), 155.

manner of the stories he heard from his parents and grandparents, with fantastic features told with straight faces alongside accounts of family history.[13]

The struggles of not just family but gender inform his novel, as Marquez admitted his view of the sexes comes out in *100 Years* and other works, namely "that women uphold the social order with an iron hand while men travel the world bent on endless folly, which pushes history forward;" the conflicts of an originally matrilineal culture with the influx of a hierarchical European society and the resulting machismo is a continuing tension in the everyday Latin American life depicted.[14] Otherwise, Marquez's main claim in the sprawling story is that the obsession with pride in all its forms, whether of power or love, eroded the ability to love and their very humanity, resulting in a solitude broken only by humility. As Lewis declared in his space trilogy, set on the gender-significant planets Malacandra (the very male

---

[13] Gabriel Garcia Marquez, "About the Author" in *One Hundred Years of Solitude* (New York: Harper Perennial, 2006), 8.

[14] "Women: Three Interviews by Plinio Apuleyo Mendoza" in *Gabriel Garcia Marquez: The Last Interview and Other Conversations* ed. David Streitfeld (Brooklyn: Melville House, 2015), loc. 509. Digital edition.

Mars), Perelandra (a feminine and procreative Venus), and Tellus (earth, with a theme of marriage from the opening word), "humility is an erotic necessity."[15] Lewis further claims that gender relations are ultimately symbolic of deeper, magical one might say, spiritual reality, in which "what is above and beyond all things is so masculine that we are all feminine in relation to it," though here on earth "obedience and rule are more like a dance than a drill - specially between man and woman where the roles are always changing."[16] Superheroes need more than their superpowers, they need the humility which turns their powers towards love and service rather than to self.

SOUL: MOMENTS OF JOY AND A FAR-OFF COUNTRY

Disney's *Soul*, while set in America, tells a story much like that of Disney's *Black Panther* (2018) or even Paramount's *Coming 2 America* (2021), namely the struggles of Africans in the modern

---

[15] C.S. Lewis, *That Hideous Strength* (New York: Scribner, 2003), 146.

[16] Ibid., 146, 313.

world.[17] *Black Panther* showed Africans as capable and advanced, yet wise and compassionate as Wakandans sought to offer their blessings to all Africans spread abroad (and the world in general); like so many Disney films reviewed here, it also showed women as capable and intelligent. In *Hamilton*, the immigrant-themed Broadway production, both racial empowerment ("But we'll never be truly free until those in bondage have the same rights as you and me," the Revolutionary Laurens declares) and female empowerment ("I'm a compel him to include women in the sequel," Angelica retorts to Thomas Paine's *Common Sense* and Thomas Jefferson's declaration that "All men are created equal") are stressed.[18] [19] Both *Black Panther* and *Hamilton* were reviewed in *An Unexpected Journal*'s Fall 2018 "Courage, Strength and Hope" themed issue.[20] Paramount's *Coming 2 America* is

---

[17] *Soul*, directed by Pete Docter (Walt Disney Pictures, December 2020).

[18] Lin-Manuel Miranda, "The Schuyler Sisters," *Hamilton* I.5, (United States: Atlantic Recording, 2015).

[19] Miranda, "My Shot," *Hamilton* I.3.

[20] Seth Myers, "Tales of Courage and Hope: Black Panther in Middle Earth and Narnia," and "Tales of Courage and Hope: Hamilton in Middle Earth and Narnia" (parts one and two) can be found in *An*

a story of remaining loyal to oneself, as King Akeem's American son Lavelle ultimately, like Akeem as a young prince, leaves Zamunda to pursue his own course; it also shows female empowerment, as Princess Meeka, like Jasmine in *Aladdin*, finally garners her father's respect enough to be given rule of the kingdom instead of being married off to a foreign prince.

Soul takes a more subtle path in depicting the issues facing African Americans. Set in New York City and featuring aspiring jazz musician Joe Gardner, a high school music teacher waiting for his opportunity, *Soul* shows the problems of young African Americans aspiring to jobs and careers unavailable to their ancestors. Joe falls into a manhole and finds himself in the "Great Beyond," where he is unwilling to proceed to death so escapes to the "Great Before," where souls are prepared for life. Joe is mistakenly assigned to mentor 22, a timid soul unwilling to engage life.

Joe strikes a deal in which he will help 22 find her "spark," her character traits and purpose,

Unexpected Journal Fall 2018, Vol. 1 Issue 3, Fall 2018,
https://anunexpectedjournal.com/archive/v1-issue-3-fall-2018/.

which she will then give him so he can return to his life (his body is in a coma in the hospital), and she can return to "living her non-life" in her comfortable routine. In their existential journeys, Joe manages to return to Earth, but 22 ends up in his body while he inhabits a feline sidekick. This begins 22's journey to finding her spark, which becomes a process of not simply determining an ultimate purpose (such as Joe's lifetime ambition to a professional jazz career) but of finding joy and meaning in the everyday moments of life, including simple pleasures like pizza, lollipops, and enjoying Joe's gift of appreciating and performing music. While 22 advances her sense of life, Joe retreats in his, slowly realizing that his career obsession caused him to miss the beauty around him. The film ends when Joe coaches 22 through his big opportunity, performing in a local jazz club, after which he realizes an emptiness to the experience and realizes how much he valued teaching young and struggling musicians. 22, however, is finally ready for the adventure of living, and she finds a way to begin hers while Joe returns, wisened and joyful, to living himself.

Soul offers wisdom that transcends a particular cultural experience, but it is also suited for the African American community. The moral feels like that of the Thornton Wilder play *Our Town* (1938), in which a young Emily Gibbs of turn-of-the-century Grover's Corner, New Hampshire, after dying while giving birth, returns to earth for the day of her twelfth birthday. Emily dwells on the beauty of living life moment by moment, bemoans how so much of life resembles that of Marquez's *100 Years of Solitude* with people "trampling on the feelings of those about [you] . . . spend[ing] and wast[ing] time as though you had a million years . . . always at the mercy of one self-centered passion or another," and asks "Does anyone ever realize life while they live it . . . every, every minute?" which receives the answer "No. Saints and poets, maybe . . . they do some."[21]

But the choice "to work to live" over that "to live to work" is highly relevant to current generations of African American youths, claims critic Timothy Thomas. Citing director Pete Docter's post-production comment that "as wonderful as these projects are, there's more to living than a singular passion" and "sometimes the small insignificant things are what it's really all

---

[21] Thornton Wilder, *Our Town*, 1938.

about," Thomas balances the purposive thrust of such popular books as Rick Warren's *Purpose-Driven Life* with the need to find meaning in everyday moments for those of us struggling with simply paying our bills. [22] This contrasts starkly with the theme of sacrificing love for career in the youthful *LaLaLand*.[23] The message is particularly relevant for young African Americans, Thomas claims, as their generation is tempted by career opportunities denied to that of their parents and grandparents.

Director Docter only came to realize this once the decision was made for the film to be cast around jazz, a uniquely African American phenomena. Like life, improvisational jazz music does not always follow a script, an insightful metaphor. Jazz's improvisation also symbolizes how African Americans "have historically found a

---

[22] Timothy Thomas, review of *Soul* directed by Pete Docter, Walt Disney. "Soul and the Purpose-Driven Generation," *Christianity Today*, last modified January 15, 2021. accessed March 29, 2021, https://www.christianitytoday.com/ct/2021/january-web-only/disney-pixar-soul-purpose-driven-generation.html.

[23] Seth Myers, "Lewis in LaLaLand." *An Unexpected Journal*, Vol. 1, Issue 2,

Summer 2018. https://anunexpectedjournal.com/archive/v1-issue-2-summer-2018/.

way to make a way out of no way, and make good against the odds, whether turning the worst parts of the pig into soul food, the worst urban conditions into a billion-dollar-a-year rap music industry" or in the successes built upon the Negro League baseball, "the beauty of black people is in the ability to be unwanted and still create gold."[24] Thomas further observes that the tension between Joe and his mother, between his dreams and her pushing him towards a full time, paying job, resonates with today's young African Americans, adding that they often have to pay a higher sacrifice to achieve the same standard of living as others.

The problem of a culture finding its true voice, the lesson that Joe and 22 learned together, is repeated throughout the postcolonial literature coming from Africa. Chinua Achebe's critically acclaimed African trilogy (*Things Fall Apart* (1958), *No Longer at Ease* (1960), and *Arrow of God* (1964)) follows an Igbo tribe in precolonial Nigeria as European steelers arrive in the late nineteenth century. *Things Fall Apart*, its title derived from a

---

[24] Timothy Thomas, "Disney's Soul is So Good Because It's So Black," *Christ and Pop Culture*, January 14, 2021. https://Christandpopculture.com.

W.B. Yeats' poem, is the signature work of the series, centered on the heroic struggles of a wrestling champion and warrior, Okwonko.[25] Okwonko is flawed, being unkind and cruel to his own family, but he defends his tribe's traditions against the newcomers. When violence escalates and Okwonko is arrested, he begins to realize that traditional forms of resistance (acts of war) are becoming passe, and finally kills himself rather than face a colonial court. Okwonko thus embodies the struggle between tradition and modernity, and he shows how a hero can have both good intentions and personal flaws. Achebe repeats this theme of the hero trapped between two cultures when he explores the ironies of twentieth century life in postcolonial Africa in *A Man of the People* (1966) and *Anthills of the Savannah* (1987). Other postcolonial African writers can be found in the Barbara H. Solomon edited *Other Voices,Other Vistas: Short Stories from Africa, China, India, Japan and Latin America* (2002).

---

[25] W.B. Yeats, *Things Fall Apart*, 1919. www.poetryfoundation.org/poems/43290. Achebe's title comes from lines 3 (and 4) "Things fall apart; the centre cannot hold; / Mere anarchy is loosed upon the world." Accessed May 30, 2021.

Literature from North Africa explores the same bi-cultural struggle but with a greater use of fantastic elements. North African sociologist and novelist Abdelkebir Khatibi claims there is a liminality, a space between, indigenous and invading (Western, colonial) cultures where meaning must be found; this theme echoes throughout his sociological work (*Multiple Maghreb*, 2019) and novels (*Love in Two Languages*, 1990, *Tattooed Memory*, 2016). Khatibi's novels throb with the fantastic, as turbulent ocean waves embody the instability of living in between two cultures and of a romance between a French woman and Arabic man. Fellow Moroccan novelist, once a philosopher, Tahar ben Jelloun uses fantastic characters from both Argentine fantasy author Jorge Luis Borges and *The Thousand and One Nights* in his novel *The Sand Child* (1985) to confuse any traditional, Western form of narrative.

While various works of postcolonial literature call into question the difference between cultural and enduring values, the lessons of *Soul* speak loudly. Just as Joe and 22 needed to learn to engage life as it came rather than imposing their plans on it, so do historically marginalized, now postcolonial, cultures feel the need to often resort to their own experience and forms of wisdom rather than those imposed on them. The truths will be the same, but it helps to see them expressed in one's own language; the face may change, but the name remains the same. They can follow Wilder's moment-by-moment relishing of life and beauty, following Ecclesiastes 3:11 which declares that "God has put eternity in our hearts," though even that may be insufficient. Lewis found that such moments could provide the clue to a deeper, more enduring meaning. William Wordsworth found that momentary joys sadly vanished, as he tried in vain to recall the face of his deceased infant daughter in his poem *Surprised by Joy*, which Lewis took as the title for autobiography. [26]

Lewis, however, found that the pangs of joy he discovered in certain moments were merely hints of something more enduring, of an ideal country of which he could only dream. "In speaking of this desire for our own far-off country . . . [it is] a secret we cannot hide and cannot tell . . . because it is a

---

[26] William Wordsworth, "Surprised by Joy" in *Poems*, 1815. accessed March 29, 2021, http://www.poetryfoundation.org/poems/50285/surprised-by-joy

desire for something that has never actually appeared in our experience" and "we cannot hide it because our experience is constantly suggesting it;" we simply "call it beauty and behave as if that settled the matter."[27] Wordsworth could not solve this puzzle, he simply sought "to identify it with certain moments in his own past" Lewis declares.[28] Instead, Lewis argues that "the books or music in which we thought the beauty was located will betray us if we trust to them; it was not in them, it only came through them, and what came through was longing;" the things themselves, if "mistaken for the thing itself, turn into dumb idols, breaking the hearts of their worshippers."[29] Instead, Lewis found that all such moments and objects, "if idolatrously mistaken for Joy itself, soon honestly confessed themselves inadequate," saying :Look! Look! What do I remind you of?"[30] Lewis learned that what he sought was not Joy, but a Person, that of God. After his

---

[27] C.S. Lewis, "The Weight of Glory" in *The Weight of Glory and Other Addresses* (New York: HarperOne, 2017), 30.

[28] Ibid.

[29] Ibid., 31-32.

[30] C.S. Lewis, *Surprised by Joy* (San Francisco: HarperOne, 2017), 268.

conversion, he came to view the momentary joys of life as mere signposts, they "were valuable only as a pointer to something other and outer," though "when we are lost in the woods the sight of a signpost is a great matter."[31] What does this have to say for the heroism of Joe and 22 who seek meaning in the moments of beauty in life? The search for such beauty is but a first step. The heroics of modern day Africans and African Americans, caught between two cultures, can show true nobility as well as the inevitable human flaws we all possess. Whatever wrongs can be righted, however, are merely hints of a far-off country which, as Lewis reminds us, is a secret but one suggested by experience everywhere.

ALADDIN: THE MAGIC OF HUMBLE VOICES

The history of *The Thousand and One Nights* shows it as a representative and beloved compilation of Middle Eastern tales, despite its relatively late discovery. The *Arabian Nights*, the title given to the first English language edition compiled between 1706 and 1721 upon discovery by French archaeologist and orientalist Antoine

---

[31] Lewis, *Surprised by Joy*, 291.

Galland, originally had just a few hundred tales, though more have been collected over the centuries to literally fulfill its title regarding the 1,001 nights during which Scheherazade told tales to the ruler Shahryar to forestall his practice of marrying a virgin each night then killing her in the morning. The tales are primarily of both Persian and Indian origin, though stories with Arabic, Egyptian, and Mesopotamian origins are included. They were first compiled in Arabic in the early eighth century in the Golden Age of Islam (the eighth through the twelfth centuries A.D.) under the title *Alf Layla* or *The Thousand Nights*, and later expanded and titled *The Thousand and One Nights*, becoming popular in the eleventh and twelfth centuries. [32]

As it grew up in an Arabic culture infused with Islam, certain aspects of *The Thousand and One Nights* reflect Islamic theology: the "thousand" in the title references the notion of infinity, so that the book is cast an infinite book, resonating with not just its large number of tales but also with how the Qur'an is considered a special, holy book

---

[32] *Great Literature of the Eastern World,* ed. Ian P. McGreal (New York: HarperColllins, 1996), 470.

delivered from heaven to the prophet Muhammad. Further, the belief in Allah's (often mysterious) omnipotence as well as the Islamic tendency to invoke angels in their cosmology encouraged the sense of the marvelous and strange, which "represent[s] a distinctive feature of Muslim thinking in the Middle Ages," found throughout the tales.[33]

The story of *Aladdin's Wonderful Lamp* (as it was originally titled), as portrayed in the 2019 Disney film *Aladdin*, exhibits some of the best aspects of Arabic culture.[34] At the beginning of the movie, Aladdin acts as a Robin Hood of sorts by giving a pouch of food to a poor, hungry street family, followed by the princess giving bread cakes to hungry children; these stories reflect the Islamic tradition of alms-giving for the needy. The story continues in its critique of greed and riches when the genie summoned by Aladdin warns against using the three wishes for "tons of money and power -- ahahahahahaha [remember, this is a

---

[33] Ibid., 473. The belief in angels is one of the six articles of Islamic faith, and jinns (genies), neutral spirits which may or may not obey Allah, occur in the Qur'an over two dozen times.

[34] *Aladdin*, directed by Guy Ritchie, (Walt Disney Pictures, May 2019).

giant, jolly, blue Will Smith as the Genie] -- do not drink from that cup, trust me, there's not enough money and power on earth for you to be satisfied."[35]

The critique of the powerful, following magical realism's propensity to express alternate rationalities and emergent cultures, is further evident in both the medieval story and the Disney film, as Aladdin struggles to survive as a street thief among the established and powerful merchants. Aladdin and Princess Jasmine both also recognize how good rulers, like Jasmine's assassinated mother, the Queen, are beloved by the people. But the greatest of all these stories is that of love, between the humble and (after a round of riches intended to woo Jasmine) chastened Aladdin and the Princess with a commoner's touch, though it is a modern love, not one of arranged marriages that her father, the Sultan, intends.

Jasmine is the first of many strong, capable, and intelligent Disney female lead characters seen here. In the film's signature song, she declares, "I won't be silent, you can't keep me

---

[35] *Aladdin,* 2019.

quiet, won't tremble when you try it, all I know is I won't go speechless," and later exercises her voice in pleading with the house guard to overthrow Jafar and save her people from his tyranny.[36] Jasmine was intentionally cast as more fully dimensional than her counterpart in the 1992 animated Disney film of *Aladdin*. Aladdin's character arc follows the *Arabian Nights* theme decrying greed, as he distinguishes himself from the scheming Jafar of similar humble origins, but who is wanton and inhumane in his pursuit of power. Aladdin also exhibits his street smarts and ennobling humility throughout, tricking Jafar and releasing the genie from his spell of eternal servitude. Together, each brings life and a voice to the traditional roles in which they find themselves, honoring the values governing them, though they do find the traditional roles can be stifling. Jasmine and Aladdin each admit they feel constricted by expectations into which they are born, and this (heroic) struggle between self and society drives the story.

---

[36] Alan Menken, Benj Pasek and Justin Paul, "Speechless," performed by Naomi Scott in *Aladdin* (Disney Pictures, May 2019).

Other themes in traditional Scheherazade's stories include adventures with themes of life and death, God's omnipotence and omnipresence, morals, universal virtues such as generosity, piety, love and faith, and the vicissitudes of destiny and fortune. *The Seven Voyages of Sinbad* and *Ali Baba and the Forty Thieves* in the *Arabian Nights* collection exhibit many of these themes. *Ali Baba* is most similar to Aladdin, demonstrating the evils of greed as the poor, younger brother Ali Baba ends up with all the riches of the forty thieves originally discovered by his older, greedy brother. Modern versions inspired by *Arabian Nights* reflect these themes as well, particularly Egyptian Nobel Prize winner Naguib Mahfouz's novel *Arabian Nights and Days* (1979) and Salman Rushdie's *Two Years Eight Months and Twenty-Eight Nights* (which add up to 1,001; 2015). Mahfouz's collection of stories is intended as a sequel, complete with such characters as Scheherazade, Shahryar, and Aladdin, but is rife with statements critical of the powerful and inhumane; recent stories indicate that it has become a political football and may possibly become banned in his home country. Rushdie's version includes humanity re-affirming values such as compassion and justice while battling battalions of evil genies; it also includes a philosophical debate between the Arabic philosopher Averroes (also referred to as Ibn Rushd, a proxy for Rushdie's own critical, rationalistic views of religion) and the famous Islamic theologian Al Ghazali.

Middle Eastern superheroes such as Aladdin and his modern inspirations exhibit not just a sense of justice but of compassion and humility as well. The importance of both compassion and family is present in *Aladdin*, and is implicit as the pretext for justice in the various other stories in *Arabian Nights* and its modern interpretations. Arabic and Islamic culture, as is most any culture in comparison to the West, is noted for its close family structure. It is a primary example of an honor-shame culture, a concept originally taken from anthropologist Ruth Benedict's study of Japan, in contrast to Western cultures characterized by a sense of guilt and justification, likely a product of the heritage of law and order from Western style democracy and political Liberalism.[37] The gospel can be easily cast in

---

[37] Ruth Benedict, *The Chrysanthemum and the Sword* (New York: Houghton Mifflin,1946). In it, she described Japan as a shame

honor-shame terms rather than the guilt-justification terms in which it is usually presented, noting that God wants to honor us by including us in His family, removing and redeeming any shame from ill done deeds. Remembering the theological basis of family from the Latin American *Coco* discussion above, Islam, translated as "submission to God," is best fulfilled when one moves from a servant of God (as followers of Allah are described, though Christians use the term as well) to a member of the family of God, heirs and joint heirs -- brothers and sisters -- of God with Jesus as Paul declared, and as friends as Jesus put it. Superheroes need families.

MULAN: TRADITIONS ON TRIAL

Mulan, like Disney's *Aladdin*, is a remake of an earlier Disney animation (*Mulan*, 1998), and like

---

culture and America as a guilt culture. Renowned missiologist Paul G. Hiebert discusses this in other cultural contexts, such as the Middle East, in *Anthropological Insights for Missionaries* (Grand Rapids: Baker Book House, 1985). The Book of Romans in the Bible is noted for its guilt and justification passages, such as how "the wages of sin is death but the gift of God is eternal life through Jesus Christ," (Romans 6:23) though it can be considered that the gospel was thus being communicated in a guilt-justification context for a society in which law was paramount.

Aladdin, retells an ancient story with an emphasis on a courageous leading lady.[38] *Mulan* is based on the legendary story (the historicity of which is a matter of debate) of Hua Mulan from the 4th to 6th century A.D., who took her aged father's place in being conscripted by the army, disguised herself as a man, and distinguished herself in combat before declining promotion then returning home. Mulan is a heroine who is not just courageous and capable but who honors family, tradition, and country, though she begins the story as a boyishly adventurous girl who chafes at her mother's plans to groom her primarily for marriage. Her father is her advocate, however, rhetorically asking his ancestors if he could tell his daughter, whose "chi, the boundless energy of life itself, speak[s] through her every motion" that "only a son could wield chi, that a daughter would risk shame, dishonor, exile?" and declaring that he could not, as he presents his version of the legend of Mulan.

Citing the values of loyalty, bravery, and truth, Mulan declares that "it is my duty to protect my family" when she volunteers as her father's son (he

---

[38] *Mulan*, directed by Niki Caro, (Walt Disney Pictures, September 2020).

has only two daughters) when she realizes his poor health will not allow him to survive conscription in the army raised to defend against the barbarian forces of Bori Khan from the north. Mulan's heroic choice, in honor of family and country, contrasts with that of the witch Xian Lang, who fights for Khan in his assault on the Emperor since he offers her the chance to exercise her powers without being vilified. When the emperor presents Mulan with an honorary sword, he adds to the virtues of "loyal, brave and true" that of "devotion to family" in a very traditional vein of Confucian filial piety and duty. Such filial duty, however commendable, is best enabled by tapping into the divine source of sacrificial love. In *The Four Loves*, Lewis describes the simpler forms of love, that of affection, friendship, and erotic love, as preliminary to that of unselfish "gift-love" or charity. But it is only Divine gift-love (charity) that is "wholly disinterested and desires simply what is best for the beloved," as mere "natural Gift-love is always directed to objects which the lover finds in some way intrinsically lovable," and will thus always be in some way selfish.[39]

---

[39] C.S. Lewis, *The Four Loves* (New York: Harcourt, 1991), 128.

Disney caters to not just traditional Confucian values, but to the Taoist thought which guided the force of the Star Wars saga. Mulan is advised by her commander to respect the fundamental force of the universe, "the chi [that] pervades the universe and all living things," with which "we are all born." Just as Samson's strength came ultimately from his obeying his vow to God, Mulan's results from her respect of the (impersonal) chi, as "only the most true will connect deeply to his chi and become a great warrior" and will be "tranquil as the forest, but on fire within" and thus "yields to the force and can redirect it [so that] four ounces can rule a thousand pounds." Augustine once declared this spiritual contentment to be the result of finding peace with God Himself, famously claiming "my soul is restless, and finds its rest in You."[40] More recently, in his journey to faith, Lewis once felt he had discovered the principle of vitality in the force of life, the *elan vital* which figured so prominently in the philosophy of Henri Bergson. Declaring that "Bergson showed me" the meaning of the word *life*, Lewis came to "relish energy, fertility, and

---

[40] Augustine, *Confessions*, I.1.

urgency; the resource, the triumphs, and even the insolence of things that grow" after which he "became capable of appreciating artists . . . resonant, dogmatic, flaming, unanswerable people like Beethoven, Titian (in his mythological pictures, Goethe . . . and the more exultant Psalms."[41] However, Lewis soon came to realize that he had come to revere just "one Divine attribute, that of necessary existence" though "it was attached to the wrong subject; to the universe, not to God."[42]

The story of Mulan, in its Disney incarnation, extends Chinese tradition to a modern world in which women can challenge any gender-wise stereotypes of the heroic.[43] The greatest novel of China, *Dream of the Red Chamber*, challenged those very Chinese traditions three centuries earlier. Written by Cao Xueqin in the eighteenth

---

[41] Lewis, *Surprised by Joy*, 242.

[42] Ibid, 250.

[43] Mulan: Rise of a Warrior produced in China by director Jingle Ma and Starlight International Production Group in 2009, showed Mulan continuing in the army and becoming a general, becoming weary of war and long travels away from home before returning to care for her ill father, and sacrificing her love interest's offer of marriage since his arranged marriage to a foreign princess would ensure peace for the kingdom.

century, like *Mulan* it shows capable women and youth coming of age on their own terms rather than those of their parents. It also questions the traditional teachings of Confucius, Buddhism, and Taoism, as well as the assumed superiority of wealth and status. It is thus distinguished from "the countless morality tales that are common in Chinese fiction," and was even discouraged reading until later in the twentieth century.[44] A complex work whose themes, images, and characters are popular cultural currency even today, the novel portrays two branches of the aristocratic Chia family in Beijing in the mid-eighteenth century. One branch centers around the boy Baoyu whose ill-fated love (so determined in heaven before birth) for a cousin not of his family's choosing leads him to become a monk, while the other branch involves another cousin of his, the irresponsible and lecherous Chia Lien who marries a capable and responsible girl, thus providing "some of the most colorful and horrifying episodes in the novel."[45] Family tensions, implying a critique of the Confucian filial

---

[44] *Great Literature of the Eastern World,* 148.

[45] *Great Literature of the Eastern World,* 148.

order, is thus a dominant theme, as is that of the Chinese "Heaven," the world beyond, as represented by the key characters of a Daoist monk and a Buddhist priest. Bayou himself embodies the conflicts, as he prefers poetry and frolics with friends over rigorous study of Confucian values and the demure wife chosen for him. While *Mulan* continued *Aladdin*'s embrace of strong female characters while still promoting values esteemed by the traditional culture, *Dream of the Red Chamber* prepared the way for *Mulan*, but questioned more thoroughly the traditions and beliefs which Disney chose to simply but effectively represent. *Dream of the Red Chamber*, however contrary to traditional Confucian commitments to filial piety and duty, paved the path for modern day Mulans who are courageous and capable while yet committed to family and country. But we can claim that the ultimate source of the strength needed by modern day Mulans is the Divine rather than Nature, the Creator rather than the creation, that allows the most pure and unselfish charity for family, friends, and country. Superheroes need a Divine source of power.

RAYA AND THE LAST DRAGON: TRUSTING SOUTH/EAST ASIAN CHILDREN SHALL LEAD THEM

Raya is Disney's conscious effort to engage the various cultures of Southeast Asia, set in the fantasy land of Kumandra, inspired by cultures of Southeast Asia.[46] [47] The featured song appeals to worldviews of various East and South Asian cultures, all influenced by Indian, Chinese, and Muslim cultures and beliefs to varying extents, as can be seen in the chorus:

There's an energy in the water
(Taoism, as in Mulan),

There's a magic deep in our
heart (Islam has a tradition of magic,
as in Aladdin),

---

[46] *Raya and the Last Dragon*, directed by Don Hall (Walt Disney Pictures, March 2021).

[47] Specifically Brunei, Singapore, Laos, Thailand, Timor-Leste, Cambodia, Vietnam, Myanmar,Malaysia, Indonesia, and the Philippines; cultural and religious influences from both India and China can be found in Southeast Asia, and a torii, the Japanese structure which serves as a gateway to Shinto shrines, appears at one point in the film.

*There's a legacy that we honor
(honoring of ancestors, as in China
and Japan),*

*When we bring the light to the
dark (enlightenment is featured in
Hinduism),*

*Whatever brings us together can
never tear us apart,*

*We become stronger together
when we trust.*[48]

Kumandra, five kingdoms (Fang, Heart, Spine, Talon, and Tail) which separated 500 years previously when attacks by evil Druun spirits petrified much of the land, its people, and all but one of the guardian dragons, Sisu, are protected by an orb into which Sisu concentrated all her magic, guarded by Chief Benja of the Heart tribe. Benja trains his daughter Raya to guard the gem, though she is betrayed by Namaari, daughter of Chief Virana of the Fang tribe, who tries to steal the gem during a feast for all five tribes. Fighting

---

[48] Jhene Aiko, "Lead the Way" written and performed by Jhene Aiko in *Raya and the Last Dragon* (Walt Disney Pictures, March 2021).

breaks out amongst all tribes, and the gem shatters into five pieces, with each tribe getting one piece; the Druun return and petrify many from Raya's Heart tribe, including her father. Much of the story consists of the small group of Raya, Sisu, and a young boatman boy Boun retrieving pieces of the gem and developing trust. Namaari's tribe has the final piece, and Raya and Namaari must learn to sacrifice for and trust each other as well as their companions, just as Sisu had to originally trust her dragon siblings with their respective magic powers to defend Kumandra from the Drunn. Trust and cooperation among the patchwork of kingdoms and cultures symbolized is the key theme of *Raya*.

A comparison with superheroes in Indian literature seems appropriate, and there is an obvious candidate in the novel about the birth of modern India, *Midnight's Children* (1981) by Salman Rushdie. Heroes abound in this novel of the birth of modern India as all Indian children born during the first hour of India's independence, between midnight and 1 a.m. on August 15, 1947, are given special powers. The tale is a natural parallel for so many Disney films oriented to the younger generation, though Rushdie's story is much less optimistic, as infighting among the young vanguards of the New India show that the Old India and its many divisions are not so easily overcome, just as *Raya*'s Kumandra was a mishmash of kingdoms and beliefs. Divisions in India persist, between Hindu and Muslim (and exacerbated by the partitioning of Muslim Pakistan from Hindu India in 1947) in addition to the Sikh, Buddhist, and Christian communities, ubiquitous social classification known as the caste system, and the patchwork of regional states, languages and cultures which make India as diverse as all of the mythical Kumandra's Southeast Asia combined.

The main cleavage in *Midnight's Children* comes from the rivalry between Saleem, born at the stroke of midnight and empowered to communicate with all 1,001 midnight's children (his large ears are key to this power) and Shiva, born at the same time who is endowed with powerful knees (with which he can crush his foes) and skill in combat, per his namesake Shiva the Hindu deity tasked with preserving and, when necessary, destroying, the world order as righteousness dictates. Saleem and Shiva are switched at birth by a nurse Mary (with an idealistic, socialist boyfriend named Joseph, a nod to Christian imagery) so that Shiva's well-to-do upbringing is stolen by Saleem, whose natural father was not the doctor who raised him but a poor, itinerant musician. Saleem's family moves to Pakistan after the partition, loses all of his family except for his sister, loses his memory, joins the army, and is rescued by another of the midnight children, Parvati the witch, who helps restore his memory and return him to India. Saleem lives with Parvati, but refuses to marry her, so she has an affair with Shiva, a war hero, and gets pregnant.

Politics drive the story, as the Prime Minister of India, Indira Gandhi, known for corruption, uses Shiva to capture Saleem, forcing him to divulge the identities of the rest of the children for sterilization. Saleem does later marry Parvati after claiming that Shiva has been killed, and raises Shiva's son Aadam, who is gifted with enormous ears with which he can listen to his father's story. The story of Shiva and Saleem achieves a balance at the end, as Shiva becomes a wealthy war hero and Saleem is returned to the poverty of his natural father, though each are profoundly affected by their upbringing. Aadem's first spoken word, abracadabra, is Rushdie's claim that the magic will continue in the next generation of India's special children.

The magically empowered heroes of both *Raya* and *Midnight's Children,* Raya and friends possess a magic dragon and garner gems with magical powers while *Midnight's Children* are empowered at birth to seek the otherwise very American trait, unity in diversity, e *pluribus unum,* "out of the many, one." Today's world longs for the respect of diversity combined with the peace of unity, but it is not easily achieved. As we hearken back to Lewis's orchestral model, in which "the song of the Church triumphant would have no symphony" and "be like an orchestra in which all the instruments played the same note, it is a divine unity in diversity that is our model."[49] Lewis cites the Bible's promise that in heaven, each person will be given a new name "which no man knows [and of course God] but he that receives it," or as Lewis suggests, "your soul has a curious shape because it is a hollow made to fit a particular swelling in the infinite contours of the Divine substance," and that "each of the redeemed shall forever know and praise some

---

[49] C.S. Lewis, *The Problem of Pain,* 155.

aspect of the Divine beauty better than any other creature can."[50] [51] Lewis directed much of this particular discussion towards Hinduism, the religion of India which has spread throughout much of Southeast Asia. In Hinduism, the individual soul eventually is lost as it gets subsumed in the cosmos, which is considered divine.[52] The cosmos into which the Hindu soul ultimately gets subsumed, and that of the Christian deity who created and "caused things to be other other than Himself that, being distinct, they might learn to love Him, and achieve union instead of mere sameness."[53] Superheroes need to learn to get along, respecting each other's unique endowments while joining in an orchestra for Divine purpose.

---

[50] Revelation 2:17.

[51] C.S. Lewis, *The Problem of Pain*, 152, 154.

[52] Hence the term *pantheism*, though care must be taken since there is an almost innumerable variety of beliefs subsumed by the term Hinduism. Historically, the belief in a pantheistic unity of existence as taught in the Upanishads followed the more ancient teachings regarding sacrifices and rituals from the Vedas, and has been superseded to some extent by the way of devotion (Bhakti), in which devotion to a particular deity (typically Krishna) assures release from the karmic cycle of infinite rebirths to achieve purity. Winifred Corduran's *Neighboring Faiths: A Christian Introduction to World Religions* is a good resource.

[53] C.S. Lewis, *The Problem of Pain*, 156.

Spirited Away: Refinding One's Humanity and One's Name

Hiyao Miyazaki's Studio Ghibli animations of Japanese life have given pleasure to viewing audiences in Japan and worldwide since 1985; their universal appeal is attested to by the annual series of Studio Ghibli animations that are played in American theaters. *Spirited Away* (2001) is the second highest grossing anime film in Japan of all time, and five Studio Ghibli productions are among the list of the top ten most popular anime in Japan.[54] *Spirited Away* is considered anime fantasy, but its frequent use of spirits and fantastic developments in a modern setting qualify it for the genre of magical realism. As often occurs with the magically realistic, escape to the countryside and nature serves as a critique of modern urban life; as with so much Eastern art and poetry, as well as with the native Shinto religion, *Spirited Away*, turns to nature and its spirits for redemption. Miyazaki anime are renowned for their beautiful, scenic depictions of the countryside accompanied by serene, joyful music; modern

[54] *Spirited Away*, directed by Hiyao Miyazaki (Studio Ghibli, July 2001).

urban environments, by contrast, though depicted exquisitely, are often breeding grounds for discontent, squalor, and disharmonious living.

Spirited Away illustrates the same themes as many of the Disney films just discussed, namely the use of fantastic elements and powers to aid the heroic protagonist in their quest for justice and values which can be found within traditional culture. The story begins as ten-year-old Chihiro and her parents move to a new home in the country, their return to indigenous, rural Japanese life amounting to a critique of modern living from the start. They have not left behind the voracious ways of modern life, however, as her parents greedily indulge themselves on a feast intended for the spirits, which turns them into pigs. Loss of identity will become a risk to Chihiro as well. Chihiro's mother appears non-Japanese, if not Western, and is thus a symbol of alien cultural influence (a stronger association with the Biblical imagery of the world system represented by the feminine figure,whore of Babylon, in Revelation 17:5 might even be justified). Chihiro finds herself separated from her parents and is lured into an exquisite looking bathhouse run by the witch Yubaba, where she becomes trapped in the spirit world and learns that she must work to be able to eventually return her parents to their human state. Chihiro's own identity is at risk, as Yubaba erases the memory of her family name and renames her Sen; her guide Haku explains that he has forgotten his own proper name, without which a person is unable to return to the human world. Chihiro encounters a spirit named No-Face, who represents a dehumanization resulting from greed, as it magically produces and offers gold nuggets to arouse the greed of nearly all the characters, then grows in size and power after it devours them one by one.

Besides the critique of the greed of modern living and a call to a more natural, indigenous way of life, *Spirited Away* invokes nature spirits otherwise prevalent in Japanese religion, known as *kami* and representing both forces of nature and ancestral spirits. This is common in Japanese literature from the ancient *Tale of Genji* to Murakami's magical realism, but for Miyazaki it provides the primary agent for redemption. Upon arrival at the bathhouse inhabited by various spirit beings, Chihiro encounters a "stink spirit," the spirit of a polluted river which cleanses itself by vomiting up an entire junkyard Chihiro's own guide, the boy Haku, is eventually helped by Chihiro to remember his own identity, which turns out to be that of the spirit of the Kohaku River, and he helps Chihiro eventually escape with her parents, vowing to find her again.

Spirited Away is not unique among Miyazaki films, nor in Japanese literature, in promoting innocence, absence of greed, the enchantment of nature (though often inhabited by spirits both good and bad), and the redemptive power of community and friendship. Other Miyazaki films illustrate such themes, as *My Neighbor Totoro* (1998) is the story of a nature spirit that nurtures children whose mother is gravely ill, *Princess Mononoke* (1997) involves a war between nature spirits and resource-scrounging humans while featuring capable female lead characters, and *Grave of the Fireflies* (1988), *Porco Rosso* (1992), and *Howl's Moving Castle* (2004) critique war and promote the values of friendship and community. Such values can also be found in traditional Japanese literature, as *The Tale of Genji* (c. 1008 A.D.) can illustrate.

Written by Lady Murasaki around 1008 A.D., the sprawling fifty-four chapter novel portrays the romances, politics, and psychology of the low-ranking prince Genji as he maneuvers his children into positions of emperor and empress. In contrast to contemporary Disney and Studio Ghibli works, women in *The Tale of Genji* are portrayed in traditionally passive yet refined and elegant manners, for which they were desired; this helped feed into a Japanese "cult of beauty" among the aristocracy "who valued beauty so highly that they turned almost every pastime into art."[55] Allied with this was the use of nature as "the dominant metaphor for artistic expression and human sentiment throughout the novel," reflecting the Japanese emphasis on nature, beauty, and its seasonal transience; the passing of the seasons also reinforce the Buddhist belief in the cycles of lifetimes. Thus the orange blossoms and other flowers of spring and summer, complimented by the foliage of autumn and the deepening red of its maple trees, are typical of the Japanese sense for beauty and precariousness of life. Thus, the much-heralded natural beauty of Miyazaki's anime and his persistent environmental themes are deeply rooted in Japanese tradition and belief

---

[55] *Great Literature of the Eastern World,* 300.

Prolific Japanese novelist Haruki Murakami demonstrates how magical realism and the fantastic can be used to bring us back to very human values; along with Marquez, he is the most prominent writer in the genre today. In *Hard-Boiled Wonderland and the End of the World* (1991), personal memories and identities may be traded for bucolic, country bliss, while in *Kafka on the Shore* (2002) characters search for meaning amidst the Japanese mishmash of humans, spirits, and nature which surfaces in *The Tales of Genji* and in the Shinto belief in divinely enchanted locales (*kami*).[56] Murakami's epic length novel *1Q84* (2009-2010) continues the societal critique of the magical realism genre, as magical "little people" represent the corrosive forces of cult religions (in contrast to George Orwell's "Big Brother" of government bureaucracy), and patricidal themes critique and combat toxic, culturally entrenched masculinity.

---

[56] John Updike. 2005. "Subconscious Tunnels: Haruki Murakami's dreamlike new novel." *The New Yorker Magazine,* January 24, 2005, www.newyorker.com/magazine/2005/01/24/subconscious-tunnels.

Other Japanese writers likewise poise their heroes to defend traditional culture and values against modernity. Izumi Kyoka's masterpiece *The Monk of Mount Koya* (1900) featured an enchantress (symbolic of old Japan) who bewitched various peddlers (merchants of the new, modernizing Japan) and turned them into animals, and Nobel Prize winner Kenzaburo Oe's *The Game of Contemporaneity* (1979) parallels Marquez's mythical traditional community of Macondo with a remote Japanese village, founded by rebels from the ruling Tokugawa shogunate, and thus critiquing modern Japan.

Two Christian Japanese authors show how traditional Japanese values of harmony and beauty can be redeemed by the gospel. Ayako Muira's *Shiokari Pass* (1968) is one of her several novels in which she explores both human depravity and sacrificial forgiveness.[57] *Shiokari Pass* is her retelling of the story of the revered Christian Masao Nagano from sixty years prior, who sacrificially supported his invalid wife and fellow countrymen. Nagano's life illustrates

---

[57] Ayako Miura, *Shiokari Pass*, translated by Bill and Sheila Fearnehough (Singapore: OMF Books, 1987).

Jesus's statement of heroic self-sacrifice, that "unless a grain of wheat falls into the earth and dies, it remains alone; but if it dies, it brings forth much fruit."[58]

A more complex, historical story of redemption is offered by Shusaku Endo's *Silence* (1966, also a 2016 film by Martin Scorsese featuring Andrew Garfield and Liam Neeson). *Silence* depicts the faith of two Catholic priests left in Japan during the Tokugawa shogunate (1603 - 1868), a period of national isolation from the colonizing European powers as well as of persecution of the Christian community. The significance is explored by writer and artist Makoto Fujimura's *Silence and Beauty: Hidden Faith Born of Suffering* (2016). Fujimura explains that the traditional Japanese notion of a different public face (*tate-mae*) and one's true, private voice (*hon-ne*) derived from this period of persecution in which one kept silent about their faith. In *Silence and Beauty* he also argues that embedded in the silent suffering which hints at one's true, private voice is embedded in the Japanese concept of beauty. The popular

---

[58] John 12:24.

aesthetic notion of *wabi sabi*, the beauty of aging things, can also illustrate this beauty born of suffering, despite the concept's origins in Buddhist teaching regarding the impermanence of life. The heroes in *Silence* are fallen heroes at best, Jesuit priests who must publicly renounce their faith to prevent the persecution of local Christians but still hold to their beliefs privately. Between Muira, Endo, and Fujimura, the noble virtues of sacrifice born of compassion and forgiveness leading to redemption exhibit a divine beauty and harmony in the living out of the Christian faith. Heroes need the qualities of endurance and sacrifice, but as they are yet mortal and fallen, they also need forgiveness and redemption to exhibit a greater harmony and beauty than they can create or preserve on their own.

SUPER AND HEROIC LESSONS FROM ACROSS THE GLOBE

Like Superman in search of an evil villain, we have crossed the globe; like Bill and Ted, we have visited many lands and learned from many heroes. Goodness and the virtues can be found, and should be found, in every culture. Where does such virtue and goodness come from? We can only point to the image of man, free from exploitation and exploiting, individuals honoring and serving their families, nations, and humanity in general; it is man made in the image of God we seek.

Just as Lewis showed in his *Abolition of Man* that virtue pervades every culture, and just as he claimed that when the poetic, noble Logres of the mythical King Arthur rules Britain, and when the order of Heaven is truly followed in China that spring will arrive, so it is with every culture. In the ancient world, the Apostle Paul once stated that "God, who said "Let light shine out of darkness," made his light shine in our hearts to give us the *light* of the *knowledge* of the *glory* of God in the face of Jesus Christ:" the Greeks valued knowledge, the Romans glory, and the Jews light, so that in the face of Christ each culture found their fulfilment.[59] One might even consider Jesus's own words when he claimed "I am the *way*, the *truth* and the *life*" that could be construed to be speaking to the Chinese (Confucius and Taoists speak of *The Way*), Greeks (who valued knowledge), and Indians (with their doctrine of

---

[59] II Corinthians 4:6, ESV.

reincarnation or many lives). Heroes and superheroes are at their absolute best when they follow the divine hero, Jesus of Nazareth, the Christ.

FAITH ON TRIAL IN FRANK MILLER'S DAREDEVIL COMICS

Clark Weidner on Questions of the Greater Good

The first published *Daredevil* comic ends with a sketch of Matt Murdock — a blind man with heightened physical senses, a lawyer by day, and a vigilante by night — looking out the window of a city skyscraper while thinking of his deceased father. Above Murdock's head is a thought bubble that reads, "Dad, wherever you are . . . I kinda hope you're resting easier now."[1] The silhouette of Murdock's shadow on the wall outlines his horn-headed, crime-fighting alter-ego, Daredevil. The image foreshadows the tumultuous journey Murdock would face as both a man of the law and a man who bends the law to stop crime. Nevertheless, it was writer Frank Miller who first shed light on many of Murdock's personal

---

[1] Stan Lee, Jack Kirby, Bill Everett, Steve Ditko, *Daredevil #1* (Marvel, March 31, 1964).

conflicts. Miller's version of the hero was pushed to the brink of introspection, trying to solve moral dilemmas and bring an end to crime while upholding the law and living out his Catholic faith. Over the entirety of Miller's *Daredevil* run, Murdock's faith would consistently shape his identity as a vigilante whose moral code is consistently tested by an ever-present evil.

Frank Miller pointed out the paradox of the men in tights who live as if they are above the law. In *Frank Miller's Daredevil and the Ends of Heroism*, Paul Young described Miller's work as unique for its time:

> Miller was not making superheroes more realistic in the way that, say, Alan Moore and Dave Gibbons [creators of The Watchmen] confronted vigilantism with real-world physics, politics, media, and sexuality. Rather, he was exploring the internal makeup of the superhero genre, poking around for contradictions and paradoxes, with the similarly stylized "realist" genre of crime fiction as his probe.[2]

---

[2] Paul Young, *Frank Miller's Daredevil and the Ends of Heroism* (New Brunswick, NJ: Rutgers University Press, 2016), 13.

Miller's version of Hell's Kitchen (the city Daredevil protects) is full of these "contradictions and paradoxes" that created internal turmoil for Murdock. Just a few examples include the fact that Murdock, a devout Catholic, must decide if he should let his enemies live, even though they may continue to kill innocent people. In one issue he must work with a villain and mob boss, Kingpin, to achieve a greater good. In another, he attempts to suppress feelings for his first love and deadly assassin, Elektra Natchios, to bring her to justice. It's these dilemmas that give such psychological and moral depth to Miller's *Daredevil* comics and brought the initial wave of attention from Marvel fans.[3]

Despite Murdock's internal tensions, his Catholic faith remains constant. Frank Miller, a self-described atheist, once said that Daredevil was the "most Christian of heroes."[4][5] Miller's run didn't typically showcase religion within the

---

[3] See Paul Young's *Frank Miller's Daredevil and the Ends of Heroism*, 8.

[4] See Frank Miller's contribution in *9-11: Artists Respond*, vol. 1 (Milwaukee, OR: Dark Horse/Chaos!/Image, 2002), 64-65.

[5] Sean Howe, *Marvel Comics: The Untold Story* (New York: HarperCollins, 2012), 241.

dialogue as often as other *Daredevil* comics, but it remained an ever-present characteristic of Murdock's conscience. Paul Young writes, "As a devout Catholic, Miller's Murdock believes in the metaphysical thermodynamics of sin: the sinner is held to account by a higher power and must atone for each sin committed in turn by embracing Christ, admitting fault, and paying penance."[6] Young's description of Murdock's metaphysical reality is a recurring theme even if it is not explicit. While Miller rarely wrote scenes of Murdock giving confession (as is so often portrayed in the popular Netflix series), nor used faith as a focal point of plot development (at least until Miller wrote the *Born Again* series which is much more religious in scope), when it came to making life and death decisions, Murdock left judgment to God and refused to murder even the vilest criminals.

Despite having a moral compass regarding murder, it could be said that Daredevil is the worst version of Matt Murdock. Murdock is a lawyer who solves problems by the book and operates within the same rules as the common man, while

---

[6] Paul Young, *Frank Miller's Daredevil and the Ends of Heroism*, 72.

Daredevil does whatever needs to be done to ensure justice. When the mask is on, he bends the law to his will so that victims will be protected and avenged. Frank Miller once said, "I see Matt Murdock as being a grown man and Daredevil almost being a boy . . . He believes in everything he's doing and he works very hard at it, but part of him just gets off on jumping around buildings."[7] Indeed, Daredevil seems to enjoy showing off his abilities for spectators. For example, in issue #170, Daredevil races an elderly man across a rooftop and leaps off the building in acrobatic fashion. The man quips, "I can't match that act, horn head!" To which Daredevil replies, "You're doing fine, Pop!" as he glides to the next rooftop.[8] While a hero leaping across buildings is astounding, Murdock's utilization of the criminal justice system is nobler.

Daredevil's boyish qualities extend beyond just playing superhero in the night; he is also a hero still coming to terms with his tragic childhood experiences. Miller pointed out the

---

[7] Peter Sanderson, "The Frank Miller/Klaus Janson Interview," in *Daredevil by Frank Miller and Klaus Janson Omnibus,* eds. Al Millgrom, Mary Jo Duffy, Denny ONeil, and Tom Defalco (New York, NY: Marvel Worldwide Inc., 2016), 781.

[8] Frank Miller and Klaus Jansen, "Daredevil: #170", in *Daredevil Omnibus,* 222.

difference between Daredevil and Batman in regards to their being orphaned by criminals. In an interview with Richard Howell, Miller says, "Daredevil operates on a basic motive of love for seeking out justice . . . [Batman] is punishing those who killed his parents. Batman's focus is on the criminal, Daredevil's on the victim."[9] The depiction of a character who's not nearly focused on revenge as he is preventing injustice seems to undercut the impact of the death of Murdock's father. Miller adds that the death of Jack Murdock (Matt Murdock's father) did not have "as big of an effect on [Matt] as his father's life."[10] Jack Murdock, a boxer, who used violence to pay the bills, once lashed out and struck young Matt Murdock in the face for getting into a fight at school. Jack's desire to see his son apply himself to something besides violence drove Murdock to go to law school but his father hitting him and eventually dying with ties to the mob made Murdock a victim let down by the man who was supposed to protect him. Without overanalyzing the impact Jack's death

---

[9] Richard Howell and Carol Kalish, "An Interview with Frank Miller," *Comics Feature* 14 (December 1981): 24.

[10] Sanderson, Frank Miller/Klaus Jasen Interview" in *Daredevil Omnibus,* 782.

had on Murdock, it's clear his father shaped his understanding of justice.

While Murdock's focus on victims is consistent with Christian charity, Daredevil is often tempted to indulge in violence. Psalm 82:3 says, "Give justice to the weak and the fatherless; maintain the right of the afflicted and the destitute." This biblical principle is embodied quite well by Murdock the lawyer, but when Murdock dons the red suit he feels the need to indulge in punishing the wicked, which cuts against the idea of forgiving your enemies. Young argues that Murdock's defense of victims is driven by his disappointment in his father's brutal nature. Young writes,

> His choice to enforce the law, both officially and unofficially, was his response to a father who first dished out brutality and then fell victim to it . . . [Daredevil] admits to his most fearsome enemy that he became Daredevil not to fulfill the legacy of his father but to correct him - to discipline him and others who threaten harm to Matt.[11]

---

[11] Paul Young, *Frank Miller's Daredevil and the Ends of Heroism*, 58.

Murdock wants to rescue victims but the devil on his shoulder tells him to be both defender and punisher, creating a temptation to execute violence beyond necessity.

Despite the conflict waging within Murdock, his faith at least prevents him from ever taking the lives of the criminals he wishes to punish. Perhaps no one tests Daredevil's desire to kill more than his nemesis Bullseye, the man with a perfect aim, for whom anything can be used as a weapon. Frank Miller made Bullseye into a deadly villain willing to kill anyone yet obsessed with killing Daredevil. It might be fair to say that if Murdock is an agent of the law, Bullseye is an agent of chaos. For example, in issue #169, Bullseye goes mad and violently attacks civilians due to a hallucination in which everyone around him appeared to be Daredevil. Murdock had to make a choice: he could uphold the law, not only of the justice system but of God by refusing to murder Bullseye, but doing so would mean Bullseye kills more innocent people. In the aforementioned issue, he rescues Bullseye from the tracks of a subway train, much to the objection of a police lieutenant. His reasoning for saving Bullseye is due to his faith in God and the justice system. Daredevil tells the lieutenant. "I wanted him to die, Nick. I detest what he does . . . what he is. But I'm not God . . . I'm not the law . . . I'm not a murderer."[12] This is a moment early on in Miller's *Daredevil* comics where Murdock's faith is strong and consistent. However, during Miller's run, Murdock's violent tendencies will be exploited and he will at least attempt to kill Bullseye, demonstrating a shift towards taking matters into his own hands.

Throughout Miller's *Daredevil* comics, it becomes clear that Murdock's faith and his moral virtues are also challenged by Elektra Natchios, his former colleague and lover at Columbia University. After the murder of her father, Elektra made it known that "I cannot continue to study laws in which I no longer believe."[13] Unlike Murdock, Elektra chose to become a deadly assassin, and his hope for her redemption always blinded him when it came to bringing her to justice (Young points out, the parallel of a blind

---

[12] Frank Miller and Klaus Jansen, "Daredevil: #169", in *Daredevil Omnibus*, 218.

[13] Frank Miller and Klaus Jansen, "Daredevil: #168", in *Daredevil Omnibus*, 185.

lawyer and blind justice "is not subtle").[14] The great pitfall of turning a blind eye to Elektra's sins is that she eventually had quite the body count, including her murder of Ben Urich, an innocent reporter and beloved character of *Daredevil* fans. It's when Elektra dies at the hands of Daredevil's nemesis Bullseye that we see the greatest change in the hero's ethical judgment. In issue #181, he drops Bullseye from a telephone wire, attempting to kill him. As Bullseye plummets for what looks like several stories, Daredevil says, "You'll kill no one . . . ever again,"[15] making clear his intentions to finish his foe. Young writes, "Here Daredevil's Christian charity gives way to ruthlessness . . ."[16] Matt's love interest causes him to overlook her murderous intentions, leaving him heart-broken and bloody-handed. Thus, his revenge against Bullseye exposed the darker side of a conflicted vigilante.

---

[14] Paul Young, *Frank Miller's Daredevil and the Ends of Heroism*, 79.

[15] Frank Miller and Klaus Jansen, "Daredevil: #181," in *Daredevil Omnibus*, 502 .

[16] Paul Young, *Frank Miller's Daredevil and the Ends of Heroism*, 122.

In the end, Frank Miller leaves readers with Murdock committing to never take a life and accepting the terms of that decision. In the last issue of Frank Miller's initial *Daredevil* run, Daredevil sits in a hospital room with Bullseye and a loaded gun. On the cover of this final issue is the subtext: "How does a man search for his own soul?"[17] In this scene, Daredevil looks deep into his own soul by playing Russian roulette with a bed-ridden Bullseye. While taking turns putting the gun to his and Bullseye's head, he begins asking a series of rhetorical questions such as "Am I fighting violence or teaching it?"[18] Finally Daredevil makes the statement that sums up his role as a crime-fighter refusing to kill his enemies: "When it comes to that one final, fatal act of *ending* you . . . my gun has no bullets. Guess we're stuck with each other Bullseye." This final panel of Miller's initial *Daredevil* run is bleak but from a Christian perspective, it shows a final, redemptive step in Murdock's journey. Murdock is no longer the man that dropped Bullseye from the

---

[17] Frank Miller and Klaus Jansen, "Daredevil: #191," in *Daredevil Omnibus*, 731.

[18] Ibid., 747.

telephone wire in an attempt to murder him and have his revenge. Instead, he has recovered the moral virtue of refusing to kill. True, Murdock is still a conflicted, flawed hero questioning his purpose, but he seems to have at least remembered why life is intrinsically valuable.

Frank Miller's deconstruction and reconstruction of his hero is what makes Murdock so fascinating. Daredevil is relatable to all of us who haven't been affected by gamma radiation or weren't born on the planet Krypton because he's human. Young noted the significance of Murdock's complicated psyche, saying, "Miller's *Daredevil* is the only creator run I can remember on a comic book in which the ultimate climax hinges not on the hero saving the world but on the hero realizing who and what he really is beneath his own idealism."[19] Matt's idealism is impacted by the complications of love, hatred, and everything in between. This development of Matt's prior notions of justice demonstrates that it's important to fight for the oppressed even if we have to mature along the way. If he were just a

---

[19] Paul Young, *Frank Miller's Daredevil and the Ends of Heroism,* 122.

hero executing justice flawlessly, he wouldn't be a person in need of redemption, he would be a god. But as Daredevil himself pointed out, he is "not God."[20]

When considering Christian themes within Miller's canon, it's worth mentioning that Miller returned to *Daredevil* with a short series titled, "Born Again." True to the title, in this volume Daredevil is given new life after losing everything. At the beginning of "Born Again," Murdock's ex-girlfriend Karen Page is a drug addict, and Murdock is isolated from the world; he is poor, jobless, and weak in body. After being stabbed to the brink of death, he's rescued by a nun named Maggie who turns out to be his long-lost mother. Maggie saves his life by taking him into a convent and nursing him to health. While fretting over the possibility of Murdock's death she prays, "He will die. But he has so very much to do, my Lord. His soul is troubled. But it is a good man's soul, my lord. He needs only to be shown your way, then He will rise as your own and bring light to this poisoned city. He will be as a spear of lightning in

---

[20] Frank Miller and Klaus Jansen, "Daredevil: #169", in *Daredevil Omnibus*, 218.

your hand, my Lord. If I am to be punished for past sins, so be it. But spare him. So many need him. Hear my plea."[21] In many ways her prayer is reflective of Christ-like suffering because she's willing to take on the punishment for Murdock's sin. Isaiah 53:5-6: "But he was pierced for our transgressions; he was crushed for our iniquities; upon him was the chastisement that brought us peace, and with his wounds we are healed." Maggie's love for her son was so great that she would be willing to suffer in his place so that he might fulfill his purpose.

Miller's *Born Again* volume also includes another Christian theme worth mentioning: Murdock learns that he never possessed any power that other humans can't access. Murdock's mentor, a blind man named Stick who trained him in martial arts, gives him a final lesson: that he's not superhuman. Murdock's ability to fight crime even though he is blind stemmed from a radar sense, which he always thought was unique. The image of the radar illustrated in the comics was an attempt to illustrate Murdock's

---

[21] Frank Miller, John Romita Jr., and Bill Sienkiewicz, "Daredevil: #230", in *Daredevil by Frank Miller Omnibus Companion* (New York: NY, Marvel Worldwide Inc., 2016), 177.

heightened senses. After an explosion, Murdock thought he had lost this radar sense. When he approaches Stick for help, he is told that he never was uniquely gifted in the first place. Young writes, "Stick reveals to Daredevil that his powers are not superhuman at all but basic potentials that everyone has. The accident that triggered his abilities did not mutate his senses or load him up with radar sui generis." Young adds, "This is where Miller leaves Daredevil: aware at last that he is not unique and stripped of whatever part his physical singularity played in his faith that he and he alone is above the law."[22] The last step in Murdock's evolution was one of humility. The person who believed he was supremely gifted in a way that no other man was, came to realize that he has always been simply human.

While Frank Miller was not himself religious and although much of his work was rife with controversy,[23] he revitalized a hero who

---

[22] Paul Young, *Frank Miller's Daredevil and the Ends of Heroism*, 91.

[23] In Paul Young's book, *Frank Miller's Daredevil and the Ends of Heroism*, he addresses the backlash to Frank Miller's comics that have been labeled misogynistic, xenophobic, and endorsing of lawless violence. See Paul Young, *Frank Miller's Daredevil and the Ends of Heroism*, 9-10.

desperately needed a new identity. Critics of Miller have good reason to disavow his more distasteful work but *Daredevil* may not have survived without him. At least we know its production was in steep decline before his arrival.[24] Miller's *Daredevil* success can be attributed in part to the trials of Matt Murdock. Furthermore, an essential component of Murdock's character is the constant test of his faith and virtue. All in all, readers can be satisfied that Matt Murdock learns who he is -- a flawed Christian trying to make sense of defending the weak in the presence of persistent evil.

---

[24] See Paul Young's *Frank Miller's Daredevil and the Ends of Heroism*, 8.

ANSWERING JOKER'S DARK-KNIGHT-DEFYING ANARCHY

Jason Monroe on Competing Worldviews

Christopher Nolan's *The Dark Knight* deservedly garnered rave reviews: in addition to the creative script and comfortable balance of action to inaction, the late Heath Ledger's performance as Joker was rightly recognized as remarkable. His masterful acting is not the whole story; Joker's ideology is powerfully demonstrated in his "interview" with Batman in the interrogation cell. Batman's forceful attempt to extract information from Joker fails as Joker replies, "You have ... nothing to threaten me with — nothing to do with all your strength."[1] The option of leveraging something of value to Joker disintegrates because he (according to the sagacious butler, Alfred), isn't "looking for

---

[1] *The Dark Knight*, directed by Christopher Nolan (Legendary Pictures, 2008), DVD.

anything logical like money. . . . Some men just want to watch the world burn."[2] There are even times when Joker is staring death in the face and simply laughs.

What can mere strength do with someone who values not even his own life? The interrogation scene shows both characters pushed to the limits of what their respective philosophies allow. Since Joker comes out ahead in this pivotal confrontation, it could be argued that he has out-philosophized Batman. Ostensibly, his position is superior and he has outwitted the Bat! But applying the law and basic sanity to his behavior, it is clear that Joker's demented, chaotic worldview is not exactly a shimmering example of goodness. We must ask, then, 'How does Batman fall short?' If a superhero is to rally any kind of following worth having, he should have a philosophy worth holding. Let's see if we can find the chinks in Batman's muscle-driven vigilantism and posit something better before the Crown Prince of Crime has the last laugh.

---

[2] *The Dark Knight,* 2008.

J. Monroe   *Answering Joker*

Apparently, "reckless abandon" accurately describes the core of Joker's mentality. Batman often strikes fear in villains' hearts because even they hold something dear (money, power, security, etc.). But having nothing to lose is a game-changer. The essence of Joker's unique confidence is his metaphysical anarchy. G.K. Chesterton captures the heart of anarchy with an analogy: "It is not anarchy in the home if the whole family sits up all night on New Year's Eve. It is anarchy in the home if members of the family sit up later and later for months afterwards."[3] Chesterton illustrates that anarchy is not necessarily disgruntled, grubby men in smokey pubs plotting insurrection. Along with opposing rules and rulers, it is a spirit of unbridled limitlessness in thought and action: "Anarchy is where you cannot stop yourself."[4] For Joker, there is no inherent or utilitarian reason to cease his momentary pleasure — no duty necessarily to preserve or destroy anything in particular. He simply wants an immediate surge of excitement

---

[3] G.K. Chesterton, *Eugenics and Other Evils* (Project Gutenberg, 2008), chap. 2, Digital edition.

[4] Ibid.

and the intoxication of "sending a message" of chaos.[5]

Attempting to pick apart Joker's pathology, one philosopher hypothesizes, "Let's suppose that his current insanity is best understood as an inability to form second-order desires to quell his first-order homicidal tendencies."[6] In more conventional terms, Joker's conscience is nearly shot. It is beyond our present scope to scour his past for the origins of his madness. But in the *Arkham Asylum* story, therapist Ruth Adams opines, "He can only cope with that chaotic barrage of [sensory] input by going with the flow . . . . He sees himself as the lord of misrule, and the world as a theatre of the absurd."[7] In typical existentialist fashion, Joker lives as if *existence* in an inherently senseless world precedes *essence* and allows him to create himself however he pleases.

---

[5] *The Dark Knight*, directed by Christopher Nolan, 2008.

[6] Christopher Robichaud, in *Batman and Philosophy*, ed. Mark D. White (Hoboken, NJ: Wiley & Sons, 2009), 79.

[7] Quoted in Sarah K Donovan and Nicholas P. Richardsom, in *Batman and Philosophy*, ed. Mark D. White (Hoboken, NJ: Wiley & Sons, 2009), 134.

Conversely, Batman's worldview has values: he supports social order and usually reinforces law enforcement. He upholds respect for basic human dignity, and according to Mark White, "Of course, with the exception of his very earliest cases, Batman has refused to kill at all, usually saying that if he kills, it would make him as bad as the criminals he is sworn to fight."[8] After all, he must have at least a decent grasp on morality to identify crime as he inspects the news or surveys Gotham from the Batcave.

But there are elements about Batman's practices that reveal his limits, restrictions, or even contradictions. He must not display weakness and he can be compromised if villains threaten his loved ones. Villains can and have gained leverage over his actions, as in *The Dark Knight* when he must suspend his fight against Joker to save Rachel Dawes, whom Joker drops out of a window. Batman's vigilantism is also suspect since he claims to bring criminals to justice, yet operates above and around Gotham City's laws. While corralling criminals, he often wantonly

---

[8] Mark D. White, in *Batman and Philosophy*, ed. Mark D. White (Hoboken, NJ: Wiley & Sons, 2009), 6.

destroys property while employing overly-invasive search and interrogation procedures. The ace up Joker's sleeve is that he defies — by refusing to be confined to — the limiting rules and structures of Batman's worldview. In other words, Joker relishes that "Batman's ultimate enemy is chaos."[9]

Our answer to this conundrum begins with a picture of a valley with a dark slope and a light slope, the dark being gradations of evil, and the light being gradations of good. Joker stands atop the dark side, since we place his worldview among the most consistent and unanswerable evils. Batman stands only halfway up the light, given his flawed — yet mostly good — principles. The point is that Batman must ascend further to approach a worthy antithesis to Joker's anarchy. This is the case because the only worldview potent enough to counter a careless, wild negation of meaning and value is one of supreme truth, goodness, and beauty. To be ideologically unassailable, Batman needs, in addition to strength and the long arm of the law, spiritual security and peace which only flow from pure humility and love: only reckless

---

[9] Brett Chandler Patterson, in *Batman and Philosophy*, ed. Mark D. White (Hoboken, NJ: Wiley & Sons, 2009), 53.

abandon into spiritual fullness can rival reckless abandon into spiritual oblivion.

A prime example of a philosophical foil to Joker comes from the classic, *Crime and Punishment*. The morally anarchic character, Raskolnikov, cannot be reasoned with or logically disproved. Disbelieving in God and objective value, no silver-bullet argument can convince him to believe in morality; if the metaphysical anarchist is consistent, morality is (in proper Joker-lingo) one big joke. Only the loving, compassionate Sonya can soften Raskolnikov's hardened heart as she exudes faith and spiritual light, illuminating the darkness in his soul. Every person has at least a small part of himself that responds to virtue over vice and recognizes truth over error. Some are more calloused than others, but while in the body, the grace to differentiate morally remains in every soul. Sonya's love and selflessness eventually waters Raskolnikov's withered spirit, reviving in him a valuation of mankind. Batman is unable to be this example because he is partially shackled by having to enforce his own rules of self-preservation and vigilantism.

One could object to our argument of Sonya's loving example, "How is a mere example effective? People often ignore or reject examples and Joker could simply reject the best lifestyle because it fails to tantalize him." True. However, in the end, there is something mysterious within the human spirit that not only differentiates between good and evil, but sees the superiority of good. A heroin addict knows he is trashing his health when he sees the healthy jogger pass by. Deep down, the thrill and tang of addiction binds him to heroin, even though he can still intellectually recognize his folly. In *Crime and Punishment,* Sonya's example and the kindness and tenderness she shows is the effective factor (not her arguments). A demonstration of life's inherent value and dignity precipitates Raskolnikov's confession. He is moved when she fans the fading spark of goodness deep within him.

It may be difficult to admit, but Joker's enduring popularity as a villain is probably partly because his worldview overmatches Batman's. Batman is rigid and rules-based, and such legalism can only go so far. Its efficacy fails in conflict with a devil-may-care anarchy which has nothing to lose because it values nothing other than "sending a message" of infinite, volatile lawlessness.[10] Only infinite volitional love that would die for a brother or even an enemy can be the answer to Joker's nihilism that would give its life to the void to spread the message of the void. Any argument is swallowed up in that existential monster of madness; but demonstrated love, refracted through faith, selflessness, and humility, vanquishes the monster. Admittedly, Batman would not be Batman if he were our idea of a full surrender to Goodness; yet perhaps he need not be. Remaining the Dark Knight we know, he represents the significance of human strength and laws in their own right. Be that as it may, doubtless some evils require the wisdom of something greater than mere worldly strength and law: paradoxically, "whoever wishes to save his life will lose it, but whoever loses his life . . . will find it. . ."[11]

---

[10] *The Dark Knight,* 2008.

[11] Matthew 16:25 (NABRE).

He Will Rise

Donald W. Catchings, Jr. on Nolan's Salvific Themes

Myriad comic series, television shows, movies, action figures, and other various capitalistic ventures have grossed billions on the back of the Caped Crusader. It seems nearly impossible to step into the public square without coming across children and adults alike adorned with some form of the Bat. (But on those instances in which the Winged Avenger is unseen, we must not forget he often adorns unmentionables.) In the midst of this Batman craze that has flooded the minds of so many for the last eight decades, there is one character from Gotham who has sacrificed more than even Batman, without proper recognition: one who has given so much as to be little more than a facade; one who has been pushed beyond the limits of most men; one who has trudged through the darkest dens of thieves, killers, and his own soul, yet came out renewed on the other side; the true hero under the mask. I am persuaded that it is Christopher Nolan's rendition of the Batman that most authentically exhibits this individual's true position in Gotham's saga via the salvific-triune — repentance, redemption, and resurrection — in his *Dark Knight Trilogy*. In this poem, I have endeavored to creatively unmask this thesis.

HE WILL RISE

Tragedy stains the night. A boy's world is **b**roken.
Here, a dark figure is born, winged and **a**woken,
Ever-seeking to avenge this dark night's **t**oken.

Damned by a torn soul. Blinded by his **m**ask.
A man apart, fated to a Crusader's t**a**sk.
Ready to betray his family name. U**n**holy Prince.
Knight, bent on vengeance, in need of
    repentance.

Knell! The death toll rings with a breaking shot.
Now a way must be sought for vengeance never
    got.
In the underbelly of the world, he goes out to
    roam,
Guided by heart and fear — He brings a secret
    home.
His secret, a legend, will strike fear into those
    who prey.
The Bat becomes a symbol, to keep criminals at
    bay.

Here lies the rub, the greatest joke of all,
Even this pure symbol will bring about a fall.

With him rises, violet and violent, a colorful jest,
In this game he plays cards close to his chest.

Laughter echoes — Will this Goliath catch the
    pale joke?
Laughter. The best medicine for a damned and
    weary soul.

Ruin befalls, in the night, the knights — white
    and dark.
In the mind of a saint, the jester's two-faced
    spark,
Stains and scars the tragic heroes, both white
    and dark.
Ending with a noble lie, the joke has played his
    part.

The World's Greatest Detective, retired and
    recluse.
His signal faded low. His legend hanging by a
    noose—
Effigy burning high in his hands. He must break
    loose.

With the calling of the cat, the **B**at crawls out his
    cave.
Here he'll find a bane to test his t**r**ue willingness
    to save.
Inside his mind, his heart, his so**u**l, he feels the
    burden's weight
Tearing and aching. His two-fa**c**ed strength
    fades. He's too late.
Every inch of his black façad**e** shattered, lying
    broken by fate.

Knight of the night, descending to a grave, a hell,
    a pit.
Now is the time to **w**eep, to mend, to resurrect.
Inch by inch, strength **a**rises in heart, in mind, in
    soul.
Gotham's reckoning? **Y**es, with the Bat's
    reckoning, in tow.
He, without praise, **n**ever seeking to be known,
    sacrifices more.
The Defender unmasked. Tru**e** White Knight. A
    man at peace—Reborn.
— *Deshi Basara*

EX-CULT MEMBER SAVED BY GRACE

Christy Luis on the Dangers Of False Heroes

. . . from what you have said about the Church of Bible Understanding . . . it may have begun as something from the LORD, but gradually you find that it has changed its course...as you'll find in all these cultish or semi-cultish groups . . . some person began to dominate the whole thing. In other words, instead of holding fast Christ as the head a man became the head.

- Steven Kaung[1]

Today, the Marvel Cinematic Universe is the largest movie franchise, judging by its box office revenue and number of films.[2] Superheroes were

---

[1] Steven Kaung, "Transcription of Recorded Meeting with Brother Kaung 10/2/87." (Meeting at the house of a pastor with several former COBU members. Transcribed by Cindy Beckman Simmons. October 2nd, 1987).

[2] "Movie Franchises," *The Numbers: Where Data and the Movie Business Meet*, accessed May 11, 2021, https://www.the-numbers.com/movies/franchises

also beloved in ancient times, when they were instead called "demigods." People have always loved superheroes — including the young people of the '70s, many of whom were reading Marvel's Bronze Age *Superman* comics. During the upheavals of the '60s and '70s in America, young people longed for leaders to bring peace, love, and happiness to their lives. No wonder they loved superheroes.

But all superheroes have their villains.

Enter the cult leader. Many cults did and do take advantage of the inherent human desire for *someone* to save the day. One ex-member of a '70s cult, Steven D. Zurcher, puts it this way: it starts with "a charismatic leader over young impressionable people."

Stewart Traill was just such a charismatic leader — although he didn't look much like one, as noted by Larson.

> His usual appearance has been a shaggy beard, stringy hair circling a bald forehead, military fatigues, Converse All Star yellow sneakers, a chain of brown leather pouches, a dozen colored, felt tip pens in his breast pocket, and a large round pin proclaiming "Get smart, Get saved." This is hardly the image one would envision for a

revered spiritual leader who likens himself to Elijah and hints that he may know the exact hour of the Lord's return. But then Stewart Traill, ex-atheist and former second hand vacuum cleaner salesman, is not a typical messianic cult leader.[3]

The desire for a superhero, so prevalent in the '70s, manifested in large followings for leaders like Traill. He launched "Forever Family" in 1971 before changing the name to the Church of Bible Understanding. COBU is widely understood, today, as a cult. Everyone, from the writers of Seinfeld to *Larson's Book of World Religions and Alternative Spirituality*, recognizes it as such [4][5]

But Steve and Melodi, in their early twenties during the late '70s, did not understand. In 1996, the *New York Daily News* was still writing about the cult's attraction for young people:

---

[3] Bob Larson, "The Church of Bible Understanding : Forever Family," in *Larson's Book of World Religions and Alternative Spirituality* (Carol Stream, IL: Tyndale House, 2004), 109.

[4] Linda Yglesias, "Cleaners Handle Rugs and Religion Shagging Sous A La TV'S Seinfeld," *The New York Daily News*, last modified December 8, 1996, accessed April 19, 2021, https://www.nydailynews.com/archives/news/cleaners-handle-rugs-religion-shagging-souls-la-tv-seinfeld-article-1.734162

[5] Bob Larson, "The Church of Bible Understanding : Forever Family," in *Larson's Book of World Religions and Alternative Spirituality* (Carol Stream, IL: Tyndale House, 2004).

State and local probers say the "church" which lists a second Manhattan address and three in Brooklyn in the past recruited teens as young as fourteen, many of them runaways, to clean for the glory of COBU coffers. "Members . . . worked for cult businesses and lived in the most tragically impoverished and almost inhumane conditions," said [Arnold] Markowitz, who has tracked the sect for 15 years. "If you were recruited and had a job on the outside, you had to tithe 90%."[6]

Steve and Melodi both encountered the cult soon after becoming Christians, when their spiritual knowledge and foundations were still being built. Both had been living on their own, doing drugs with friends, when they experienced something new — something real. They met their super hero, Christ.

"One of my friends stopped smoking and drinking with us and all of us thought he'd lost his mind," Steve says. "We went to talk sense with him."

But Steve's friend ended up leading him to Christ.

---

[6] Linda Yglesias, "Cleaners Handle Rugs and Religion Shagging Sous A La TV'S Seinfeld"

"I started reading John and the Holy Spirit just came into the room and illuminated the whole gospel for me. I would sit at the kitchen table reading and crying."

He spent time with a group house of young Christians, and, for a while, the experience encouraged him. He loved the times of prayer and Bible study. But his friend also connected him with a group house that was part of the cult, the Church of Bible Understanding, and the church leadership decided he "needed" to go to Philadelphia to learn more and grow. His girlfriend gave him an ultimatum: "Choose me or Jesus." He thought choosing "Jesus" meant going to Philadelphia, so in 1977, that's what he did.

So the problems began: Traill came into the picture, eclipsing the glimpse of Christ that had turned Steve's life in a healthy direction.

At first, Steve didn't question any of the proceedings. After his previous life, the regimented routine of the Church of Bible Understanding might have felt more stable. He described the routine that he experienced later, at the New York location of the cult: "We went to work, then spent three hours a night evangelizing on the streets of New York. Then we'd come back for a meeting, talk about it, pray, go to bed, sleep for five or six hours, then get up and start the day over." Steve still says, "I think it was part of God's plan for Melodi and me to be locked up in that cult. It kept us alive. Our former lifestyles could have killed us." Even today, Steve clearly still feels the pull of Traill's morally grey, yet still villainous plans for saving a generation from chaos.

Speaking in 1987 to a group of former COBU-members, Steven Kaung explained some of the cultural and spiritual context that may have given rise to cults that appealed to so many young people:

> . . . it began roughly 20 years ago. That was the time when all these young people wanted to be free[;] then out of that came the young people who wanted to find authority. First of all you find this JESUS movement and things like that, and a subculture began to develop and people just wanted to be free with no authority, no organization, throw everything away. But then a reaction came in and as a result of that you find the different groups. For instance the Children of God is one of them . . . The result is the people who are in that group begin to lose their individuality. They cannot make any

decisions because they are not supposed to and they don't want to because if someone can make the decision for you it takes all the responsibility away from you and that is easy.[7]

Traill successfully created the illusion of a safe space for the young people, setting himself up as a biblical superhero, using the prophecy about the return of the prophet Elijah in Malachi 4:5-6.[8]

In Philadelphia, Steve and the other "lambs" (new converts) or "sheep" (advanced believers) lived free of charge in gender-segregated fellowship houses and worshipped in meeting houses. The leaders provided meals, and Steve reminisces, "We used to pray together, all at once, in the meetinghouse and it would sound like a 'rumble' to outsiders. We had very enlightening Bible studies."

One of the "brothers" owned a coffeehouse and got Steve a job delivering coffee and bagels to office buildings. Later, another brother gave him a job at a construction company nailing 2 x 4s together. Steve incorporated himself into an

---

[7] Steven Kaung, "Transcription of Recorded Meeting with Brother Kaung 10/2/87."

[8] Malachi 4:5-6, NASV.

assembly line, working on a little piece of a job every day. The craftsman did the skilled labor. Steve turned his checks into the "fellowship house" and received an allowance of $2 a day or $5 a week.

But soon the COBU leaders started sending higher-ranking brothers and sisters (called "guardians" by Larson) out into the fellowship houses to assess the health of the lower-ranked.[9] These leaders decided to send Steve to New York City for more training, in early 1978 — and that's where he stayed until 1981. He was "kicked around to various houses in the boroughs, such as Queens, but he was sent back to "Hell's Kitchen" (in Manhattan) every time."

Melodi was recruited in a similar way. "Mom was brought in from Ohio," Steve says. He agrees to give me a rundown of the details, since Melodi prefers not to talk about those times.

> "The leaders there assessed her and decided she needed to be sent to New York. They put her on the bus with a few bucks and a bag of chips and she arrived

---

[9] Larson, Bob, "The Church of Bible Understanding : Forever Family," in *Larson's Book of World Religions and Alternative Spirituality*.

very starved and hungry. There, she met other brothers and sisters who assessed her according to a 'color' system. If you were judged to be 'black', you were put into the 'Trip' apartment, where you were not allowed to commingle with the rest of the members. You didn't live with them. The other colors were brown and orange; if you're brown, you're in the flesh, a bad person. If you're orange, you're one of the examples. It was very harsh."

The cult perpetuated other harsh teachings and practices, more typical of a villain's lair full of hazing lackeys than a superhero's "batcave." Rather than practicing healthy techniques, learning to use helpful tools, and building a supportive network of friends, this cult worked its members day and night, practiced public humiliation, and fostered an abusive culture of criticism within the "family."

In New York City, Steve witnessed and experienced the "spiritual abuse due to legalism" cited in *The Concise Guide to Today's Religions and Spirituality*.[10] He worked in the church-

---

[10] James K. Walker, "Church of Bible Understanding, Stewart Traill," in *The Concise Guide to Today's Religions and Spirituality* (Harvest House Publishers, 2007), 99.

owned carpet cleaning business. "I was out with my carpet cleaning machine . . . in Harlem . . . and I was mugged . . . I got back to the brothers at the end of the day to turn my machine in and told them what happened. They said I must not be taking Jesus and my life very seriously. I guess when I presented it, I didn't have the spirit they were looking for. It wasn't at all an uplifting, encouraging kind of thing." Instead of encouraging Steve by reminding him of their faith in their superhero and his power, they diminished both with their legalism.

Steve says that, over the course of his stay in New York, "the screws got slowly applied and if there was any challenge to the authority, he [Traill] would have the other older brothers take you down. Then you started thinking maybe he *is* Elijah. Your discernment got shut down. And that was when you become a cult member. . . . He had a good sense of human nature and was able to isolate you from your family and former friends. 'To follow Jesus', of course."

Traill also isolated Steve and other young members from their families. Larson explained that Traill "challenges his converts to break off all familial relationships on the premise that those over 30 (excepting Traill) are too spiritually hopeless."[11] As a case in point, Steve's sister invited him to her house for Christmas one year when he was staying in New York. Steve asked the guardians if he could go see her, and they said that wasn't a good idea. "She started to cry because she knew that it was a cult thing," Steve said.

Villains usually kidnap people; superheroes rescue and reunite those people with their loved ones. Stuart Traill's COBU clearly fits one of these arcs better than the other.

COBU guardians, and perhaps Traill himself, used other tactics to convince the "lambs" and "sheep" to stay in the fold. "Those who have left the commune report having been intimidated by suggestions that backsliders may meet a tragic end," Larson tells us.[12] Steve confirms this. First, the guardians would convince members, "there's a higher knowledge in the cult. There may be Christians outside, but they have a lower understanding. We called them 'Church

---

[11] Larson, *Larson's Book of World Religions and Alternative Spirituality*, 110.

[12] Larson, *Larson's Book of World Religions and Alternative Spirituality*, 109-110

Christians'. But *you're* responsible for what *you* know. And remember what happened to what's-his-name. He got his head caught in an elevator and died."

Eventually, Steve and several brothers started attending other Christian gatherings like the Grace Crusades by Wayne Monbleau and Bruce Morgan, and listening to speakers like Betty Baxter. Steve says he doesn't remember how he stumbled across the Grace Crusades, but that grace was certainly the key to his salvation from the cult.

"There was a prophet at the Grace Crusade whom I felt was speaking right to us. He was giving a generalized scenario to illustrate grace; his message was 'the law and grace', or something along those lines. In it, a *vacuum cleaner salesman* tried to intimidate a young man with all of his faults. We were stunned. The physical descriptions of the salesman even matched Stewart!"

Everywhere they went, people saw their "Get Smart, Get Saved" buttons and asked them, "Do you know you're in a cult?"

Steve and the brothers knew Christians like this as "Contentious Christians"; that's what the guardians called them. But Steve couldn't deny what he was feeling.

"All I knew was that when I went to that Crusade," he says, "I felt joyful. But the cult members I bumped into sensed I was different and tried to bring me back into that discouraged spirit. Because if you were encouraged and happy, it must be fake."

Some of the older men who had also experienced the Grace Crusades warned Steve to remain silent so he wouldn't become a target. Many of them did end up escaping the cult, but they knew the transition wouldn't be easy if they talked about it too much.

Steve didn't listen. Grace was a superpower he had never encountered before and he had to share it. "None of us had understood the meaning of verses like Ephesians 2:8: that Jesus Christ had saved us 'by grace'.[13] I went ahead and talked to some of the ladies about grace. I told them Jesus had done it all and that their behavior had nothing to do with if they were accepted into Christ's family."

---

[13] Ephesians 2:8, NASV.

He and a friend took Melodi out to breakfast, and they told her about grace. She started crying into her breakfast special, over-easy eggs.

But the cult didn't like it when their members started packing to leave.

> "As Melodi was packing to move out of the building where she had been housed," Steve says, "the sisters of COBU gathered together and warned her that I was 'trying to wolf her away' and that 'things were going to be very bad for her if she left'. A group cornered my friend while I was at work and grilled him for a long time until he started hanging his head. By the time I arrived, he had already succumbed and said we were wrong. It took him a few days to realize he was being coerced."

Eventually, however, they did escape. Theirs is one of the happier stories. After leaving, they took an apartment with another couple who had escaped. They joined Everybody's Tabernacle in Howard's Beach. They started their ministry of worship there, which they continue to this day. They got married at that church with paper plates, and the church paid for everything. Steve has recently spent more time reconnecting with some of his fellow members through Facebook groups such as "COBU."

Speaking sadly of a recent conversation he'd had with one of the brothers from the cult, he told me, "He still talks like we did in the cult. He still holds to a lot of the basic doctrine. He didn't go to the Grace Crusades with us, and I don't think he was ever delivered."

"Escaping a cult" means more than fleeing the physical location or turning away from a toxic group. "Humanly speaking or looking back into history, probably a great many will be just forever wrecked. It's very, very sad . . . I'm afraid you've come out of it, but it probably hasn't come out of you completely."[14]

Stewart Traill's prospects dimmed considerably, starting with the Jonestown massacre in 1978 and following other events. "The IRS put the rug-cleaning operation out of business, and the truth of Traill's divorce and remarriage surfaced: Traill, forty-six, and his wife had exchanged accusations of adultery in a messy divorce proceeding, after which he married his

---

[14] Kaung, Stephen, "Transcription of Recorded Meeting with Brother Kaung 10/2/87," 3.

COBU secretary — half his age — only 6 weeks later."[15]

Steve explains that it was Jesus who set them free with His grace. He and his friends recognized that Jesus, not Stewart, the supposed "Elijah," had the power.

Although Traill liked to pretend he was saving a whole generation from early death and Hell, he and the cult lost sight of the real superhero: Christ. Instead of pointing young people to the real hero, he tried to make himself into one. Ultimately, he became the villain.

---

[15] Larson, Bob, "The Church of Bible Understanding : Forever Family," in *Larson's Book of World Religions and Alternative Spirituality*, 109.

Super-Women and the Price of Power

Annie Crawford on Gendered Superheroes

The idea of a heroic female warrior is not new.[1] While Wonder Woman, Black Widow, and Captain Marvel have given the trope unprecedented popularity, Homer makes the first Greek reference to the ancient Amazon warrior women in his *Iliad*. Old King Priam recounts "that day when the Amazon women came, men's equals," to fight in bloody war before the walls of Troy.[2] Later, the Roman poet Virgil gives one of the greatest battle scenes in his *Aeneid* to the female warrior, Camilla, queen of the Amazons and leader of their all-woman cavalry.

---

[1] To limit its scope, this essay will only consider the symbolic meaning communicated through the most popular superheroes films and not the extended and vastly more complicated world of comic books.

[2] Homer, *Iliad*, trans. Richmond Lattimore (Chicago: The University of Chicago Press, 2011), 1.189.

Watch, exulting here in the thick of
    carnage, an Amazon,
one breast bared for combat, quiver at
    hand — Camilla — now
she rifles hardened spears from her hand
    in salvos, now
she seizes a rugged double ace in her
    tireless grasp,
Diana's golden archery clashing on her
    shoulder.
Even forced to withdraw, she swerves her
    bow
and showers arrows, wheeling in full flight.
And round Camilla ride her elite
    companions . . .
Godlike Camilla's aides in peace and war
    and wild
as Thracian Amazons galloping, pounding
    along
the Thermodon's banks, fighting in
    burnished gear
around Hippolyte,[3] or when Penthesilea[4]
    born of Mars
comes sweeping home in her car, an army
    of women

---

[3] As one of his great labors, Hercules stole the magical girdle from the Amazon Queen Hippolyta.

[4] One non-Homeric legend tells of a hand to hand combat between Achilles and the Amazon Queen Penthesiea. After Achilees killed Penthesiea, her helmet fell and Achilles fell in love with her for her great beauty as she lay dying.

lifts their rolling, shrilling cries in welcome,
exulting with half-moon shields.[5]

Camilla slaughters warrior after warrior in her own epic rampage against the Trojan men. She is only cut down herself when distracted by a desire to plunder Chloreus's gold armor and saffron cape. Focused on her loot, Camilla does not see Arruns's javelin until it rips through her flesh, right beneath her naked breast.[6]

Virgil freely gives as much strength and courage to his women warriors as to the men, but as an artist, he must work with images from the world that God created. While generously praising the might of Camilla, he still must describe her having a woman's body — and a woman's body will communicate in form what God created it to communicate — sensual beauty, fertility, and vulnerability. Two images in particular reflect the essential and unavoidable tension inherent to the idea of a female warrior hero: her breast and her

---

[5] Virgil, *The Aeneid*, trans. Robert Fagles (New York: Penguin, 2006), 11.766-782.

[6] Virgil is not here chastising Camilla for a feminine love of clothing. An inordinate desire for plunder is one of Virgil's primary themes and what leads to the downfall of several men in *The Aeneid*, including the climactic death that ends the epic.

shield. Is it not curious that Camilla and her warriors ride with one bared breast, an image reflected symbolically in their half-moon shields which betray the woman's true vulnerability through both need for lighter gear and the cut-out shape of her exposed breast?[7]

According to one of the most notorious Greek legends, Amazon women would cut off their right breast so it would not hinder speed and accuracy in archery.[8] This belief was supported by one etymological interpretation of the name Amazon, which combines the prefix "a" for "without" with "mazos" which means "breasts." Whether or not this legend has any truth to it, the symbolism is telling. For women to fight as men, it must cost them something — something essential to their God-given nature as women.

The capacity to bear life is the basis of feminine identity. A woman's capacity to hold life within

---

[7] Virgil, *The Aeneid*, 1.594. The Latin word here is the dative singular, *mammae.*

[8] The Amazon women were a popular subject of Greek visual art; however, the warrior women were never portrayed as having a breast removed. This may be explained by the well-established Greek artists' obsession with physical perfection. Certainly there was no need to portray Athena, the goddess of battle, as mutilated in any way.

herself and to nurture that new person through its vulnerable infancy and childhood requires an inherent softness that is incommensurate with the hardness of a male form prepared for battle. This means that to play the role of hardened warrior hero, a woman must in some way sacrifice the very thing that defines her as a woman. A man can step into the role of the warrior superhero without sacrificing any part of his masculinity or humanity because this is a role proper to his gendered identity as initiator and protector. He was made to lead and defend. But the more a woman takes on the role of the warrior hero, the less she can retain what essentially makes a woman a woman.

The most loved superhero movies are honest about this Faustian bargain, or what *Wonder Woman 1984* calls the curse of the monkey's paw. The worst female superhero films lie to us by trying to portray women and men as essentially interchangeable without cost, and as a consequence they ring false. Why else would we love Black Widow so much but be rather bored by Captain Marvel?

In *Iron Man 2*, Black Widow begins as a two-dimensional warrior spy whose skill set includes sex appeal, deceiving people, and beating up men. Natasha is smart, sexy, and powerful, everything both modern feminists and lazy, lustful men want a woman to be. She is an icon for the delusional male fantasy that a woman would both do the dirty work of battle for you and still want to have sex with you.[9] That's not how real relationships work, at least not for long. The idea of a beautiful, powerful female side-kick who will both take the lead in battle for a man and still find him sexually appealing is pure fantasy. This is not the way a woman's body or heart is made to work.

First, let's compare the female body to Black Widow's warrior abilities. Could a real woman, apart from the tricks of filmmaking, actually be as good a fighter as Black Widow? No. Admittedly in the Marvel comics, Natasha was given a weaker form of the super-soldier serum which gives her peak human abilities and enduring beauty, but not superhuman capacities as Captain America possessed. However, in the films, the source of Black Widow's abilities are not clear and, unlike

---

[9] For a discussion of why female warriors appeal to men, see Nathan Alberson's explanation in his "Open Letter to Rae from Star Wars" at https://warhornmedia.com/2016/03/07/an-open-letter-to-rey-from-star-wars/

Wonder Woman or Wanda or Captain Marvel, she looks to many undiscerning eyes as an image of what a real woman could possibly be.

The truth is, women are significantly weaker than men physically, and judo-styled moves are insufficient to fully equalize the playing field between Black Widow and her throngs of male opponents. While the physical difference between men and women should be and historically has been perfectly obvious, the modern flood of feminist propaganda has made such common sense observations not so common. Recent research driven by the issue of transgender women in sports has shown the physical advantages of men over women to be undeniable. Men are 7-8% taller and 36% larger than women. Their upper bodies are 40% larger with larger muscle mass and more fast-twitch muscle fibers. Male bones are longer, thicker, and denser than female bones, which means women are more prone to injury and have lower force generation and reduced kinetic mass. Men have larger lungs and hearts and 12% more hemoglobin than women, which all leads to around 30% greater VO2 max. Men lift 35% more than women in competitive weightlifting and the striking power of men is 160% greater than that of women.[10]

Black Widow is playing a role that women can't physically play, and when we live against our nature, it costs us something. What has it cost Natasha? To begin with, it has cost her her modesty. She uses sex appeal as one of her main weapons to distract, confuse, and manipulate the men to whom she is sent. The sensuality of her body is no longer a sign of life-giving love but has rather become a sign of manipulation. This too is a deal with the devil, for a woman's beauty does not remain forever, nor are all women equally beautiful. When the beauty of the female body is separated from loving, committed union oriented toward the growth of family, it becomes not a gift but an enslaving ideal. As a tool to manipulate men, a woman's beauty must be put in competition with other women. Few can win this war, and all will age and wear. But to love one man, one woman's beauty is enough.

---

[10] Gabriel A. Higerd, "Assessing the Potential Transgender Impact on Girl Champions in American High School Track and Field," *United States Sports Academy*, ProQuest Dissertations Publishing, 2021. 28313943. https://www.proquest.com/openview/65d34c1e949899aa823beec ad873afae/1?pq-origsite=gscholar&cbl=18750&diss=y

Second, let's consider a woman's heart. Women are not the only ones making a foolish Faustian bargain when they abandon traditional gender roles rooted in biology, natural law, and Scripture. When men give up their mandate to take the lead in responsibility for others, they abandon the very thing that a woman finds most attractive in a man. This is why Wonder Woman loves Steve Trevor and why his loving sacrifice is the most powerful part of her first movie. It's the reason why Jack's sacrifice for Rose made *Titanic* the first film to gross over a billion dollars. Had Rose slipped beneath the icy waters and left Jack alive, the movie would have never had the same wide appeal and cultural impact. There is a reason why the self-sacrificing male hero is the story women worldwide long to hear.

Gender relationships are made to work a certain way for two reasons. First, men are made to lead because this is how families are best built. Child bearing requires a softer, yielding body able to make a space for another human to grow within, and therefore a man must take the lead in protecting and providing for the woman so she can fulfill her more vulnerable role. We need each other. Gender difference is not the result of the fall;

it is God's original, good, beautiful design for mutual dependence, service, and love. Second, as Paul tells us in Ephesians, the gendered union between man and woman is an icon of the Gospel. The free, total, faithful, self-giving, and self-sacrificing love that a husband has for his wife embodies Christ's love for his church. Just as Christ and his Bride play different roles in the story of salvation, so men and women play different roles in their gendered lives together here on earth.

Moreover, as Lewis bluntly confesses in *That Hideous Strength,* this complementary gender dynamic is an "erotic necessity."[11] The epidemic rise of kinky fetishes, bondage motifs, and rape pornography reveals that when we remove the loving and erotic interplay between male leadership and feminine responsiveness, sex becomes dull, destructive, and crude. It is in embodying and acting out the mythos of gender that we find a natural and life-giving arousal able

[11] C.S. Lewis, *That Hideous Strength* (New York: Scribner, 2003), 146. For a full discussion of Lewis's view of gender, see my essay, "Gender and the Imago Dei: Together We Reflect The Image of God" in the Spring 2021 Issue of *An Unexpected Journal,* https://anunexpectedjournal.com/gender-and-the-imago-dei-together-we-reflect-the-image-of-god/.

to draw from an infinite well of divine love that needs not the cheap, cartoonish kitsch offered behind the desperate doors of your local adult sex shop.

Fortunately, Marvel develops Black Widow into something more than a sexualized fantasy warrior. She becomes more human and believable as her story unfolds because we discover the deeper price she has paid for her fighting abilities. In *The Avengers*, Natasha is sent to recruit Bruce Banner and a personal relationship begins to grow between them. Banner repeatedly mentions how he feels like a monster (the script rather belabors this point). His superpowers seem to have cost him his humanity — his ability to be in society and to have intimate relationships — and Natasha responds to this vulnerability. We see her drawn to Banner in a way that she is not drawn to any of the others. Neither Steve Rogers nor Tony Stark nor Thor are damaged by their powers: Bruce Banner is, and this is something Natasha understands.

In *Age of Ultron*, Natasha reveals to Banner the nature of her combat training. To become an elite espionage agent, the capstone of her training in the Red Room involved a hysterectomy — the permanent removal of her feminine capacity to home and birth new life. Bruce felt like a monster because his masculine strength had taken a corrupt form, and Natasha felt like a monster because her feminine strength had been corrupted and deformed. Black Widow's very name captures the contradiction inherent to the female warrior: her power to kill robs her of her power to have a family. Yet through her vulnerable and emotional confession to Bruce, Natasha is humanized. She reveals her deepest longings and they are wonderfully feminine; she wants a fruitful relationship with a man and it is her secret grief that this capacity has been taken away from her.

Black Widow's final moments reveal the redemptive grace in Natasha's life, for her life as a warrior ends with a reversal of the Faustian bargain that began it. To receive the power of the Soul Stone, a person must give up the one they love most — a soul for a soul. In *Infinity War*, Thanos the anti-father sacrifices his adopted daughter, Gamora, to gain the power of the stone. To retrieve the Soul Stone for the Avengers in *Endgame*, Natasha freely sacrifices her life to give Hawkeye the stone so he can return and bring back his family. Natasha began her life as a warrior by being forced to sacrifice the possibility of ever having a daughter to gain her supernatural powers, and Natasha ends her life as a hero sacrificing herself so Hawkeye might have his daughter again.

In the Marvel films, Hawkeye was Natasha's Christological hero, the one whose compassion rescued her from the KGB and the evil that enslaved her. In response to that salvation, she served throughout most of the films as a helpmate to the Avengers, using the power she was given in the fight against evil. In *Winter Soldier, Civil War,* and *Age of Ultron,* the moments that most characterize Natasha are the moments she is making space in her own heart for the sorrows, struggles, and cares of others. Despite the deceptive and corrupting message of her sexy-warrior persona, Natasha's most intimate relationships reveal a feminine soul.

Intuitively, we know that men and women are different and that women cannot fulfill uniquely male roles without sacrificing part of their femininity. This is precisely what the heart of Black Widow's story tells us and we love her for it. In the final analysis, she tells us the truth.

The recent success of *WandaVision* rests on similar grounds. Like Natasha, Wanda's deepest desires and secret sorrows are feminine. As represented by her superpowered sitcom fantasy, what she wants most is a husband and a family, and the drama of the whole series arises from the premise that her superpowers are incommensurate with the family she desires. Like Natasha, Wanda attracts us because her character deals somewhat honestly with the conflicts inherent to women warriors. Incredibly, Marvel actually taps into the truth and power of Wanda's femininity to excuse her from full moral culpability for oppressing and controlling an entire town.

Captain Marvel, by contrast, tells us very little truth about who women are and how they were made to live, which is why it is one of the lowest rated and least-loved Marvel films, despite its free pandering to the feminist ideology of the age. Whereas Black Widow resonates with us on an archetypal level because of what her powers cost her as a woman, Captain Marvel doesn't resonate with us because she never sacrifices anything to become the great lead hero of the universe. Carol's life doesn't show us the Faustian bargain a woman must make in order to become a warrior. She never wanted to be a woman in the first place.

Every flashback in the film shows us a girl who wants to be a boy — playing baseball with the boys, driving recklessly around the racetrack with the boys, training with the men in bootcamp, partying in the roadhouse bar like a man. It's not just that she wants to play baseball, drive race cars, or train on the ropes course, which would be fine; it's that she wants to do those things with the men and at the same level as the men. Her backstory is centered on her desire to be like a man, that is, to be what she isn't.

Carol's personality is primarily an anti-personality — defined by her opposition to her feminine nature. As a result, she is hard, closed, sarcastic, and egocentric. Her best friend Maria describes her as smart, funny, powerful, and "a huge pain in the ass."[12] Carol didn't get along with her family; she didn't have a romantic relationship; there is no part of Carol's backstory that tells us she values anything that is unique about being a woman or really anything else besides her own

---

[12] *Captain Marvel*, directed by Anna Boden and Ryan Fleck (Walt Disney Studios Motion Pictures, 2019), Disney Plus streaming.

ambition. Maria remembers how Carol wanted to prove herself at all costs and was always looking for her hero moment. The only way we know she is a woman is because of the shape of her body; there is nothing feminine about her personality, her desires, or the role she plays.

I am hard on Carol Travers because I am like her, and we are usually hardest on ourselves. As a young adult, I too was hard, closed, sarcastic, and egocentric, but not because I was a powerful female destined to break patriarchal stereotypes. I was unfeminine because I was broken and alone and afraid of my vulnerability. Like so many others in Generation X, I am a child of divorce, and I was hurt by the breaking of the father-daughter bond. I grew up feeling that I needed to protect and care for myself. I didn't have the strong and stable covering that would help me learn how to be safe and secure with my desires for a husband and a family. To compensate, I worked to establish my own independent sense of security by feeding my ambition, trying to prove myself, and always looking for my hero moment. If *Captain Marvel* portrayed Carol as broken, I would have compassion for her and understand her, but the movie portrays her hard, egocentric personality as a positive good. That characterization does not show me the truth. Why should we praise in Carol Danvers what we demand be broken in Tony Stark? This is narrative driven by our ideology, not our true humanity.

The film also lies to us about why Carol wasn't able to compete with the boys in baseball or boot camp; rather than be honest about the fact that the female body cannot keep up with the male body in such physical endeavors, the movie presents her as held down by misogynist attitudes.

This feminist theme is further developed through the mind control of the Kree, for *Captain Marvel* is a not-so-subtle story about deconstructing traditional gender roles. When the film begins, Carol has had her extraordinary powers for over six years, and the only reason she cannot use them is because she has been brainwashed by the Kree. Carol's Kree mentor, Yon-Rogg, controls Carol by telling her that her emotions make her vulnerable and that she must suppress them. The patriarchal, brainwashing Central Intelligence tells Carol that she is weak, flawed, and helpless — the usual lies attributed to misogynist oppression of women. But Carol, the feminist hero, realizes that by believing the lies she has "been fighting with one hand tied behind my back."[13] Now that she sees through the matrix of patriarchal lies, Carol is free to use *all* her powers. And what can a woman who is free from the patriarchy do? Anything! To prove it, Carol starts glowing all over and takes down a whole space army single-handedly, giving *Captain Marvel* the most anti-climactic, childish ending of any Marvel movie.

Fantasy is thrilling because it explores the boundaries of the possible and because magic — be it supernatural or technological — functions as a narrative symbol for the divine. We long to be lifted from the limitations and sorrows of the fallen natural world, and we know such transcendence requires participation with the supernatural. But when fantasy denies that there are *any* moral or relational limits to human nature, it goes too far and begins to deceive rather than inspire.

Captain Marvel violates our moral and relational limits in two ways. First, by taking on, as a woman, the role of lead male hero, Captain

---

[13] *Captain Marvel*, 2019.

Marvel destroys what it means to be a woman. A true feminist would not give us women who are simply free to act like men but women who show that the unique qualities and tasks of womanhood are themselves as valuable as those of manhood. We should indeed create female characters who are powerful and brave and clever, but a woman's power and courage and wit is going to be expressed a bit differently than a man's power and courage and wit because she has different capacities and different callings.

Second, Captain Marvel inappropriately violates moral and relational limits by having completely undefined and unlimited powers.[14] She is too god-like. And when powers are so great and so vague, the challenge of plotting a great story is gone. It is the limits of our powers which create dramatic tension and the need for heroic action. Even Christ took on limits when he became human and then shocked man and angel alike by defeating evil through death on a cross.

---

[14] This charge could be made against several other characters in Marvel. The franchise as a whole struggles to maintain consistent, definable laws and boundaries for its fictional world. As a result, the viewer is asked to exercise considerable suspension of disbelief, but so long as the special effects are cutting edge, it is a bargain most are eager to make.

The joyful surprise and narrative power of the Gospel comes through the way God accepted limitation and then used those very limits to shake the powers of hell and turn the world upside down. When Captain Marvel can destroy the terrifying space army in two minutes by simply flying straight through their ships like a blonde fire bullet, it's boring, and the only thing it symbolizes is the cosmic inflation of Carol's egocentric ambitions.

If Black Widow and Wanda represent the most feminine of our contemporary superheroines and Captain Marvel represents the least, Wonder Woman is the most ironic. On the one hand, the psychologist William Moulton Marston created Wonder Woman in 1943 to be "psychological propaganda for the new type of woman who should, I believe, rule the world."[15] Marston was a polygamist who openly enjoyed erotic bondage and admired the way "women enjoy submission — being bound."[16] Marston also supported Margaret Sanger's work to free women

---

[15] Christopher Klein, "Wonder Woman's Surprising Origins," *HISTORY*, last modified January 12, 2021, accessed May 17, 2021, https://www.history.com/news/wonder-woman-origins.

[16] Ibid.

from biology so they could step into their role as matriarchal leaders of a new world. He believed women could bring about a peaceful world matriarchy by teaching men "to enjoy being bound . . . [for] only when the control of self by others is more pleasant than the unbound assertion of self in human relationships can we hope for a stable, peaceful human society . . . Giving to others, being controlled by them, *submitting to other people cannot possibly be enjoyable without a strong erotic element.*"[17] In other words, Wonder Woman was created to train men to enjoy the erotic pleasure of being controlled by women who attain power through the suppression of their fertility, for Marston believed we will never learn to love our neighbor unless we eroticize that love. Marston's sexual ideals certainly give Diana's glowing rope of truth new meaning.

The initial setting for Wonder Woman presents us Marston's ideal matriarchal paradise. On the island of Themyscira, Diana's home, there is no need for men as women have all the roles

---

[17] Gerard Jones, *Men of Tomorrow: Geeks, Gangsters, and the Birth of the Comic Book* (New York: Basic Books, 2004), 210, emphasis mine.

and power that the men would have. The women warriors live in perfect peace with each other, and the first *Wonder Woman* film makes sure to let us know that sexual pleasure is still a part of their idyllic, lesbian culture. Men are not necessary to them for anything; sexual gratification included.

Themyscira is a godless island, lying to us about the nature of human relationships as well as the nature of God. Humans were created to bear the image of God in the world, both glorifying Him by showing forth His love and character in the physical world and enjoying divine relationship with Him together. This *imago Dei* is not complete without both men and women living in loving, other-oriented communities. Woman without man is a godless creation, a world with no one to create it and love it. Man without woman is a loveless god, a divine power with no one to serve or love. In the creation story of Genesis, it is the woman who represents the relational character of God and foreshadows the truth of the Trinity. The masculine alone represents a divine creator, but in order to know that the divinity is love, there must be a relational component to Him. It is not good that man or woman should dwell alone.

On the other hand, the basic plots of both *Wonder Woman* films are surprisingly faithful to these gender archetypes and honest about what it costs a woman in order to play the world's hero. The first film works well because the climax offers us a timeless heroic sacrifice. Once Diana leaves Themyscira, it is Steve Trevor who leads the adventure. He introduces Diana to the world of men, he leads her onto the battlefield, and he is the one who makes the ultimate sacrifice, dying to save his world and his love. Despite its obvious imitation of *Captain America*, Steve Trevor's heroic victory is genuinely moving because it touches on genuine truth. Christ our hero has sacrificed Himself to save His world and His bride. It is the rescue we need and the rescue we need our stories to tell us. Because of Steve's heroism, Diana is empowered to complete her own mission in a way that symbolically resonates with the work of the church. It is the love of Steve and, as we discover at the end, the power of her true father Zeus, that enables her to overcome the evil of Ares.

Moreover, the first film shows us what it will cost Wonder Woman to be the superhero savior of Earth — the one relationship her feminine heart most desires. The conflict between her desires as a woman and her identity as the world's superhero frames the primary plot of the second film, *Wonder Woman 1984*. The movie opens with a memory from her training on the island of Themyscira. She cheats in a contest and, in rebuke, Diana's mother and her aunt Antiope warn her that, "No true hero is born from lies."[18]

This anecdote sets the stage for the entire movie, which unfolds into a profoundly ironic reflection on the contradictions of the female warrior trope. The primary villain, Maxwell Lord, nearly destroys the planet by tempting people to wish for what they have not been providentially given. Enlivened by Pedro Pascal's first-rate acting, Mr. Lord depicts this Faustian bargain with flair. In exchange for the illicit power to transcend your given situation, the wisher loses their most valuable possession. Maxwell Lord loses his health to become the wishing stone, Barbra Minerva loses her kindness to become like Diana, and Wonder Woman loses her divine powers to bring back her love, Steve Trevor.

---

[18] *Wonder Woman 1984*, directed by Patty Jenkins (Warner Bros, 2020), Amazon Prime streaming.

The longer Steve stays, the weaker Diana grows. She resists renouncing her wish until there is no other hope for saving Earth. With the world on the brink of nuclear war and total destruction, Steve insists that she must let him go. Diana confesses and emphasises that this relationship is the one thing she wanted, the one thing she asks in exchange for everything she gives the world. It is a vulnerable and tender desire every woman knows. But this one thing is incompatible with the superpowers that make her the hero and leader of this narrative world. She can't have her heart's desire as a woman and be the hero. It is a moving and poignant moment of surprising truth offered in a movie made as feminist propaganda.

Diana saves the world by renouncing her false wish. In her climactic speech, she tells Maxwell Lord, "Everything has a price, one I'm not willing to pay, not anymore. You can only have the truth, and that is enough."[19] Indeed, Diana. Secular feminism has a price, one I'm not willing to pay, not anymore. We can have the truth, the truth about what it means to be a woman, and that is enough. God has made womanhood and it is

---

[19] *Wonder Woman 1984*, 2020.

good and beautiful, and I am glad to be a woman and to have a home full of daughters. My daughters and I don't need female heroes who tell us we are free to act like men. We need women characters who inspire us to love being women who act like women.

*   *   *

Author's Note: Many thanks to Nathan Alberson, Jake Mentzel, and Ben Sulser at Sound of Sanity and Sanity at the Movies for inspiring both this essay and many a good dinner conversation with my daughters. For more on the gender iconography of your favorite superhero movies, I encourage readers to start with the Sound of Sanity episode on Wonder Woman and the Sanity at the Movies episodes on Princess Leia and Wonder Woman 1984.

Diana Prince, Apologist?
Salvation and the Great Commission
in *Wonder Woman*

Megan Joy Rials on an Unlikely Apologist

When *Wonder Woman* was released, it was hailed as an audience favorite, and Gal Gadot's performance as Diana Prince was widely praised. Christian reviewers noted the Christ-like character of Diana's selflessness and specifically noted that in one critical scene, her method of defeating the main villain was similar to depictions of Jesus on the cross.[1] Others enthusiastically welcomed Diana as an illustration of the Hebrew word *ezer*, or helper, an ideal for the Christian woman to strive for.[2] Still others rightly criticized Diana for

---

[1] Suzanne Morse, "Wonder Woman: Christian allegory?" *Medium*, last modified November 18, 2017, accessed January 5, 2021, https://sznnmorse.medium.com/wonder-woman-christian-allegory-e8be413f2ee9.

[2] Marilette Sanchez, "Wonder Woman and Biblical Womanhood," *Think Christian*, last modified September 18, 2017, accessed January

her sexual ethics, or lack thereof, in having premarital sex with her love interest.[3] Here, I approach the film from a different angle. The character of Diana is flawed, but within the framework of the story, she is not presented as being perfect, and we should not look for such perfection outside Christ. The storyline readily suggests basic Christian truths, however, and in Diana, we see an inspiring example of how we as Christian apologists should approach our neighbors and the world.

"Not About Deserve": God's Unmerited Grace and the Redemption of Creation

Throughout the film, much emphasis is placed on the word "deserve." When Diana leaves the island of Themyscira to save the world from the horrors of World War I (at least, so she thinks), her mother, who kept her sheltered there, warns her

---

5, 2021, https://thinkchristian.net/wonder-woman-and-biblical-womanhood.

[3] Amy Mantravadi, "Is Wonder Woman a Good Example of Biblical Womanhood?", *Amy Mantravadi*, last modified July 6, 2017, accessed January 5, 2021, https://amymantravadi.com/2017/07/06/is-wonder-woman-a-good-example-of-biblical-womanhood/.

that "the world of men does not deserve [her]."[4] The word crops up again in a later conversation with her friend and eventual paramour, Steve Trevor. Although he tries to tell her otherwise, Diana insists that by killing the god of war, Ares, she can end World War I. After she kills the man she believes to be Ares — an evil character who would have committed more destruction had he been given the opportunity, despite not being Ares himself — the war continues, and Steve begs her to help him fight other battles. Diana balks, confused as to why the soldiers are still killing each other. Steve replies, "Maybe it's them. Maybe people aren't always good, Ares or no Ares. Maybe it's who they are."[5] Diana concludes that her mother was right, that the world of men does not deserve her help. Steve then delivers the film's most insightful lines: "It's not about deserve! Maybe we don't. But it's not about that, it's about what you believe. . . . You don't think I get it, after what I've seen out there? You don't think I wish I could tell you there's one bad guy to blame? It's

---

[4] *Wonder Woman*, directed by Patty Jenkins (DC Films, 2017), Blu-ray (Warner Bros. Pictures, 2017).

[5] Ibid.

not. We're all to blame."[6] When Diana responds that she is not to blame, Steve says simply, "But maybe I am."[7]

When he tells Diana that "maybe it's who [we] are," Steve recognizes corrupted human nature, and we see a glimmer of the truth that we are all sinners desperately in need of God's grace because of the Fall of Adam and Eve.[8] Steve is correct that there is "not one bad guy to blame": by saying he is to blame, he indicates each person is at fault, for as Scripture tells us, "all have sinned and fall short of the glory of God."[9] Similarly, each of us is to blame for the sin in this world; we make mistakes and sin, every day, in thought, word, and deed, and we are each personally responsible for the broken state of our world. Just as the world of men did not deserve Diana's help, we do not deserve God's unmerited grace in the sacrifice Jesus made for us. We deserve every thorn in the brow, every lash of the whip, and every pounding of the nail that Jesus received when He was

---

[6] *Wonder Woman*, 2017.

[7] Ibid.

[8] Ibid.

[9] Ibid.; Romans 3:23.

tortured and crucified, bearing our sin and punishment to atone for our crimes before God so that we could experience eternal life with Him.

In contrast to Diana's mother, who did not want to give her only daughter to a world desperately in need of her help, how grateful we should be that we have a God who gave His only Son willingly! We see parallels in Diana and Christ in that through a specific individual, the world is saved. Further, we may note that Jesus, in His earthly life, was located in a specific culture: that of the Jews in the first century. He is, as it were, "culture-specific" because He lived as a particular man in a particular family in a particular part of the world, and each believer must assent to His culturally specific Incarnation: in Him, divine truth is "culturally embedded."[10] As C.S. Lewis noted, Jesus embodies the "dying god" story as expressed in other mythologies, but the difference is that in Christ, the story concretizes in a specific man, a specific time, and a specific culture: "It is like watching something come

---

[10] Stanley J. Grenz, "What Does Hollywood Have to Do With Wheaton? The Place of (Pop) Culture in Theological Reflection," *Journal of the Evangelical Theological Society* 43, no. 2 (June 2000), 308.

gradually into focus; first it hangs on the clouds of myth and ritual, vast and vague, then it condenses, grows hard and in a sense small, as a historical event in first century Palestine."[11] Indeed, Jesus represents the ultimate "narrowing" of the specific way in which God worked in the Old Testament: first, by choosing the Jewish people through whom He would work salvation; then, by the "purg[ing]" and "prov[ing]" of that group over and over again, until "at last it comes down a little point, small as the point of a spear — a Jewish girl at her prayers."[12] Thus, we see that God's decision to redeem all His creation is accomplished in a highly specific and personal way: through the Incarnation of His Son, Jesus Christ, Who ministered to those around Him in a culturally sensitive manner, such as when He approached the Samaritan woman differently than He approached Nicodemus.[13] Our duty as Christians is therefore "to serve the present generation by

---

[11] C.S. Lewis, "Is Theology Poetry?", in *The Weight of Glory* (New York: HarperOne, 1949), 129.

[12] C.S. Lewis, "The Grand Miracle," in *God in the Dock*, ed. Walter Hooper (Grand Rapids: William B. Eerdmans Publishing Co., 1970), 84.

[13] Grenz, "Wheaton," 308.

speaking within and to the cultural context in which God has placed us."[14]

One significant way we can speak within and to our culture is by engaging with the artistic expressions of our day. As a result of the present-day church's tendency to overlook a theological tenet the early church father Irenaeus emphasized — that Christ came to redeem not only humanity, but the entirety of God's creation, including the natural world — we can be too quick to condemn wholesale works of art not specifically labeled "Christian."[15] If we take seriously the idea that Christ is redeeming every piece of God's good creation as we look forward to the New Heaven and the New Earth, then we must also take seriously the idea that He has redeemed art and culture — and this not only in a general sense, but in a specific sense. That is, that because of this redemption, His truth may be found in specific works of art. We may then use this truth to illuminate to our non-believing neighbors fundamental bases of Christianity, just as we are

---

[14] Grenz, "Wheaton," 308.

[15] Bengt Hägglund, *History of Theology*, 4th rev. ed., trans. Gene J. Lund (St. Louis: Concordia Publishing House, 2007), 48-49.

now doing as we analyze the echoes of Diana as a Christ-figure. Of course, not every artistic expression is somehow completely redeemed, or even redeemed in any degree, depending on the work, but we should not underestimate the power of the Holy Spirit in His influence on our culture. Here, evangelicals should particularly take note, for we are far more likely than our Catholic counterparts to view culture with suspicion: whereas evangelicals focus on the sinfulness of the world and assume God's absence from the arts, Catholics emphasize His presence and the "sacramentality of the world."[16]

RADICAL LOVE THROUGH EVANGELISM AND APOLOGETICS

After her disastrous exchange with Steve, Diana still refuses to help to him, and as a result, Steve embarks on a suicide mission to destroy weapons that could kill thousands more. The real Ares finds Diana, and during their showdown, he taunts her and suggests that she kill the disfigured German war criminal, Dr. Poison. He tries to persuade Diana that all humans are evil

---

[16] Robert K. Johnston, *Reel Spirituality: Theology and Film in Dialogue*, 2nd ed. (Grand Rapids: Baker Academic, 2006), 104-105.

and should die, telling her, "You know that she deserves it; they all do."[17] After remembering Steve's last words to her — that he loved her — and his sacrifice, Diana refuses to believe Ares, saying, "You're wrong about them. They're everything you say, but so much more . . . It's not about deserve. It's about what you believe. And I believe in love."[18]

Here, we see the Christian virtues of sacrifice and mercy, which are intimately connected with God's love. Steve's sacrifice also recalls Jesus's own sacrifice and His words, "Greater love has no one than this, that a man should lay down his life for his friends."[19] Although Diana's statement of "believing in love" is glib in that it tends toward the modern error of emphasizing God's love to the exclusion of His just wrath against sin, it nevertheless points to the radical forgiveness we experience because of God's love: "For God so loved the world, that he gave his only son, that whoever believes in him should not perish but

---

[17] *Wonder Woman,* 2017.

[18] Ibid.

[19] Matt. 15:13.

have eternal life."[20] The word "radical" has its origin in the Latin word *radix*, or root, and indeed, God's love is so deep, comprehensive, and cleansing that upon accepting Christ, we are not admitted to God's house as only servants or even guests, but instead welcomed as His sons and daughters.[21] Jesus spares us through His sacrifice and mercy, as Diana spared Dr. Poison, but He does what Diana cannot do for the disfigured doctor. Sin is rebellion from God and manifests itself through disobedience to Him as we pridefully and deceitfully attempt to make ourselves the centers of our selfish worlds. Such refusal to recognize God as Lord, King, and Creator of all — of our lives, of the universe, of eternity — results in separation from Him and His cosmic truth. Sin deforms us in every way possible — physically, mentally, and spiritually — because it is acting in defiance toward the objective moral facts and laws of God's fundamental reality in creation as they are embodied in His commandments. This mutiny dehumanizes us, for we cannot flourish as

---

[20] John 3:16.

[21] "Radix," *Merriam Webster,* accessed January 5, 2021, https://www.merriam-webster.com/dictionary/radix.

creatures made in the *imago Dei*, or the image of God, without Him. Jesus, however, heals us of sin's destructiveness, restores our humanity, and makes us part of His eternal family. This, for those who, as Genesis explains, threw away perfect union with God at the dawn of the world in exchange for revolt against our Creator and Father and the ruin of His good creation. What radical forgiveness and mercy, indeed!

There is an echo of such mercy in Diana's refusal to kill Dr. Poison, despite her chilling war crimes, which points to the forgiveness we as believers are called upon to practice. Just as God forgave us, so we are to forgive our neighbor's sins against us.[22] In Jesus's parable of the servant, the servant is forgiven by his master, but refuses to forgive his fellow servants and is condemned by his master. When Peter asks Jesus how many times the disciples had to forgive others, He replies, "Seventy-seven times."[23] If God could forgive us for the sin we have committed against Him, so much more should we forgive one

---

[22] Matt. 6:14-15.

[23] Matt. 18:21-22.

another and thereby extend God's goodness to those around us.

One of the primary ways we show our love for our non-believing neighbors is in carrying the Gospel to them through apologetics. We as Christians have a duty to love God with all our hearts, minds, and strengths, but further, we have a duty to share the Gospel — literally, "the good news," derived from the Greek *euangelion* — with our non-believing neighbors. In the Great Commission, Jesus commanded His disciples, and through them, all believers, to spread the Good News of His Incarnation, Crucifixion, and Resurrection: "Go therefore and make disciples of all nations, baptizing them in the name of the Father and of the Son and of the Holy Spirit, teaching them to observe all that I have commanded you."[24] What unmerited grace we have received in God's forgiveness and eternal life through Christ — how could we not wish to tell our non-believing neighbors about God's love and His eternal gifts so that they may also share in them? As Jesus said, who would light a lamp and

---

[24] Matt. 28:19-20.

it under a basket?[25] This spreading of the Gospel is called "apologetics" because its Greek root word, *apologia*, means defense.[26] In the Christian context, it refers specifically to giving a defense and reasons for one's belief in Jesus Christ as the crucified Son of God, Who gave His life to atone for man's sins and to offer salvation to all those who accept Him as their personal Savior.[27]

The fact that our culture has turned its back on Christianity is even more reason for us to engage. Jesus noted, "The harvest is plentiful, but the laborers are few; therefore pray earnestly to the Lord of the harvest to send out laborers into his harvest."[28] How timely are these words even two thousand years later, and how much more eagerly should we volunteer to be the laborers! We must seek to be like Paul, the apostle to the Gentiles, when he is at the Areopagus and notices among the statues of the Greek gods one marked, "To the unknown god," which he uses as a springboard to

---

[25] Matt. 5:15 (ESV).

[26] "Apologetics," *Coptic Orthodox Diocese of the Southern United States*, accessed January 5, 2021, https://suscopts.org/resources/literature/546/apologetics/.

[27] Ibid.

[28] Matt. 9:37.

explain that the Christian God is the one true God.[29] Here, we have a Scriptural model of using a half-truth embedded in contemporary culture to share the full truth as embodied in Christ. Similarly, we should not rely only on producing purely philosophical proofs for the existence of God. We can and should interact with today's cultural expressions, such as books, films, television shows, music, and theatre in our quest to use the fragments of truth they contain to show Christ to the world.

CONCLUSION

Diana destroys Ares and concludes the film by noting,

"I used to want to save the world. . . . But then I glimpsed the darkness that lives within their light and learned that inside every one of them, there will always be both — a choice each must make for themselves, something no hero can defeat. And now I know: that only love can truly save the world. So I stay. I fight and I

---

[29] Acts 17:22-31.

give, for the world I know can be. This is my mission now. Forever."[30]

Diana's words ring true: as Aleksandr Solzhenitsyn noted, "the line dividing good and evil cuts through the heart of every human being."[31] Because we are made in the *imago Dei*, we are capable of goodness, but as a result of the Fall, we are corrupted by sin. All our righteous works and acts without Jesus are as filthy rags, for we cannot earn our way into Heaven with our supposedly good works, and we cannot be "good" without Him. The standard for admission to Heaven is not whether an individual is a "good person." As C.S. Lewis notes, our "niceness" arising from our natural personalities is simply not sufficient for, or relevant to, the redemption and salvation of our souls.[32] To paraphrase Lewis, in determining whether we spend eternity in Heaven or Hell, it is not whether we are nice

---

[30] *Wonder Woman*, 2017.

[31] Cynthia Haven, "Happy Birthday, Aleksandr Solzhenitsyn!", *The Book Haven*, last modified December 11, 2015, accessed January 5, 2021, https://bookhaven.stanford.edu/2015/12/happy-birthday-aleksandr-solzhenitsyn/.

[32] C.S. Lewis, *Mere Christianity* (New York: HarperOne, 1952), 215-16.

people that matters: it is whether we are new men and women through belief in Christ. Without belief in Christ and His atoning work on the cross, we are condemned to the wages of sin: eternal spiritual and physical death, and separation from God in Hell. The only standard that counts is how bad we are compared to Christ, not how good we are compared to other people, and whether we have repented of our sins and believed in Him as our personal Savior. No hero can make such a decision for us; it is each individual's personal responsibility to choose to submit his life to Jesus. As Steve says, "It's about what you believe," and indeed, Jesus teaches that "no one comes to the Father except through me": all we have to do to receive this beautiful gift is to believe that Jesus Christ is the Son of God and that He died for each of us and our individual sins.[33] Our subsequent willing obedience to His moral commandments shows our love for Him, for as James reminds us, faith without works is dead, and our faith is shown by our works.[34] Paul explains that Christ makes each of us into a "new creation," and we are then

---

[33] *Wonder Woman,* 2017; John 14:6.

[34] James 2:17-18.

freed from the oppressive sin that enslaves us to our passions and desires.[35] Jesus redeems and transforms us to be like Him, and when we lose our lives to obedience and suffering in imitation of His example, we discover the paradox He discusses in the Gospel: he who loses his life will find it. As Jesus leads us on the road of self-sacrifice, we find our true selves in Him, for He enables us to pursue the unique callings God places upon our lives.

One significant difference between Diana and Christ is that the individuals in the film's universe need not believe in Diana or even know of her existence to benefit from her actions, for she saves only their earthly lives. In contrast, Jesus saves our souls, and simply being aware of His existence as the Son of God is insufficient to receive salvation and eternal life. As James notes, even the demons believe in God, but this kind of belief is mere knowledge does not translate into a faith that gives salvation.[36] A salvation-giving faith requires an element beyond mere intellectual acceptance of Jesus as the Son of God. It is a faith where I as

---

[35] 2 Cor. 5:17.

[36] James 2:19.

an individual trust in and have a personal relationship with Jesus as my Savior who died on the cross for my own unique sins against God, accompanied by my obedience to His commandments. Jesus is not merely a fact to be assented to or a math equation to be solved — He is our Lord who bled and died on the cross and who desires a personal relationship with each individual. It is through this relationship that Jesus's sacrifice accomplishes an individual's salvation, for in it, we each confess our crimes against God and personally accept the gifts Jesus offers us: to atone for our sins through His death and resurrection and to restore our relationship, and eternal life, with God.

Despite this difference between Diana and Christ and the Christian God's absence from the film, Diana is right that only love can save the world — indeed, it already has. God's love has rescued creation through the victory over sin and death Jesus won on the cross. Hearing these fragments of truth in films such as *Wonder Woman* reminds us of the fundamental Christian truth that we were not made for this broken, sinful world, and because nonbelievers do not have Christ in their lives, they will continue to have

Christ-sized caverns in their souls. Thus, they will continue to ask questions only Jesus can answer. Taking our modern culture's expressions seriously allows us as apologists to see what questions are being asked and how they are framed. If we do not pay attention to the specific issues troubling our non-believing neighbors, we will never hear their questions or truly address their concerns; we would be like the most tragic ships passing in the night. Instead, we must meet our neighbor's needs and answer their questions as they ask them, not the questions we think they should ask. Engaging with cultural expressions, such as film, as we have done here with *Wonder Woman*, also allows us to present the truth in a fuller manner than dry rational propositions would, for art allows us to address the whole person, not solely the intellect, and to express the meaning of our faith as well as the reasons behind it. If we hope for nonbelievers to come to faith, we must first seek to show them the joy we have in Christ.

The final lines of the film should be a challenge to every Christian. If Diana, the flawed demigoddess of the D.C. universe, is willing to risk herself for humanity, even without the promise of a Savior, we as apologists should be all the more willing to fight and to give everything for the world we know could be when it is united under Christ, to bring every thought and deed captive to Christ, and to preach the Gospel to every nation and every person, so that they can experience the beautiful gift of eternal life we have been given in Jesus. And yes, as we sort through our artistic expressions and navigate the lies of Satan and the ugliness of fallen human nature, cultural apologetics can be messy — but in this broken world, what isn't? Christ has promised to give us a New Heaven and New Earth that will come not from the replacement, but from the sanctification and renewal, of this very world. The gauntlet has been thrown down. If Jesus is willing to fight for this world, so must we. Will we leave our culture to the world's destructive devices, or will we stay and fight for our mission to spread the Good News through every means possible — now and forever?

ONCE A PRINCE OR PRINCESS: MACDONALD'S MORAL SUPERHEROINES AND HEROES IN THE PRINCESS TALES

Seth Myers on Ordinary Heroic Actions

Of all the stories I have read, including even all the novels of this same novelist, [The Princess and the Goblin] remains the most real, the most realistic . . . the most like life.[1]

- G.K. Chesterton

How do we become good or evil? . . . All these philosophers [Plato, Aristotle, Confucius, Lao Tzu, Rousseau, Thomas Hobbes] are wrong, probably because most of them do not have children.

---

[1] G.K. Chesterton, *Introduction to George MacDonald and His Wife* cited in "In Defense of Sanity" ed. Dale Ahlquist, Joseph Pearce and Aidan Mackey (San Francisco: Ignatius Press, 2011), 301.

Parents and children know the answer: by example. By having moral heroes.[2]

– Peter Kreeft

Superheroes are simply moral heroes, but with superpowers. That is not to say that, like any mortal hero, they do not have their weaknesses, faults, sins, or room to mature, but it is in their courage and moral heroism that they most live up to their credentials as Super*heroes*. In the Christian tradition (omitting all the Olympian, Norse, and other mythological warriors and gods), such heroes can be found in its imaginative literature, and for the modern era, that means George MacDonald. While his fairy tales are heralded as mythopoeic, and served as inspiration for later Christian imaginative works such as C.S. Lewis's *Chronicles of Narnia* series as well as J.R.R. Tolkien's *Hobbit* and *Lord of the Rings*, at the heart of each tale is a moral goodness not just embedded in the created world, but embodied in the characters. Nowhere else is this as evident as in MacDonald's *Princess* tales. Lewis heralded this

---

[2] Peter Kreeft, "Foreword" in Louis Markos, *On the Shoulders of Hobbits: the Road to Virtue with Tolkien and Lewis* (Chicago: Moody Publishers, 2012), 8.

goodness in his praise of MacDonald's *Phantastes*:

> The quality which enchanted me in his imaginative works turned out to be the quality of the real universe, the divine, magical, terrifying, and ecstatic reality in which we all live . . . what I learned to love in Phantastes was goodness . . . [not] that prosaic moralism which confines goodness to the region of Law and Duty, which never lets us feel in the face the sweet air blowing from 'the land of righteousness' . . . 'more gold than gold.'[3]

Just as Chesterton cited the realistic quality of the *Princess* tale -- that evil lurked just under the floorboards and must be battled -- Lewis reminds us of the glorious goodness that combats such evil in our everyday lives. Thus, while Lewis declared that MacDonald's *Phantastes* "baptize[d] my imagination," he continued to next cite how the moral component would later complete his transformation.[4]

------

[3] C.S. Lewis, *George MacDonald* (New York: HarperOne, 2001), XXXVIII.

[4] Ibid. Lewis continues by stating that "It did nothing to my intellect nor (at that time) to my conscience. Their turn came far later with the help of many other books and men."

Building on *An Unexpected Journal*'s recent George MacDonald-themed issue (Advent 2020), we examine MacDonald's *Princess* series, *The Princess and the Goblin* and its sequel, *The Princess and Curdie.*[5] In between these, MacDonald also wrote *The Wise Princess: A Double Tale* (also known as *The Wise Woman*) which is included, as it is an even more direct excursion into the moral makeup of young women who would behave worthy of the moniker (in the best sense) of *Princess*.

MacDonald's imaginative work is considered groundbreaking in not just its moralizing but in its mythmaking, as Lewis and Chesterton explain. Lewis declared that what MacDonald "does best is fantasy -- fantasy that hovers between the allegorical and mythopoeic," and "this . . . he does better than any man."[6] Lewis stated that while myths typically originated in "prehistoric times, and, I suppose, not consciously made by

---

[5] These reviews augment those of *Phantastes, Lilith, The Golden Key,* and *At the Back of the North Wind* from our MacDonald issue: "George MacDonald," *An Unexpected Journal* 3, no. 4 (Advent 2020), www. anunexpectedjournal.com/archive/v3-issue-4-george-macdonald/.

[6] C.S. Lewis, *George MacDonald*, XXIX.

individuals at all . . . every now and then there occurs in the modern world a genius -- a Kafka or a Novalis -- who can make such a story," adding "MacDonald is the greatest genius of this kind whom I know."[7] Lewis did not rank MacDonald in the first or even second rank as a literary figure, but claimed that "it was in this mythopoeic art that MacDonald excelled."[8] Lewis included these three Princess tales along with *Phantastes*, *Lilith*, and *The Golden Key* as MacDonald's best mythopoeic works. Similarly, Chesterton claimed that were he to compose a list of "Books that Influenced Me," a MacDonald book would top that list, namely *The Princess and the Goblin*. His claim that it is "the most like life" of all the stories, including others by MacDonald, that he had ever read owes to it including not just magical stairways but also "subterranean demons who sometimes come up through the cellars," emphasizing the threat from within against which a notion like Holy War pales.[9]

---

[7] C.S. Lewis, *George MacDonald*, XXXII.

[8] Ibid.

[9] G.K. Chesterton, *Introduction to George MacDonald and His Wife*, 301.

The Princess and the Goblin: Fighting the Evil Underneath and Within

The Princess and the Goblin and its sequel, *The Princess and Curdie*, are both set in the mythical, fairytale kingdom of Gwyntystorm, and tell the story of Princess Irene, her father, the King (good, wise, and widowed), and the young miner Curdie who saves Irene and her father from the plots of goblins and corrupt officials. Set in a castle in the mountains, in which are located both the mines worked by the townspeople as well as cavern homes of a race of goblins, *The Princess and the Goblin* is a story of conflict between the kingdom and the goblins. The goblins left the countryside years back over some dispute, moving underground and becoming misshapen and hideously ugly, matching their inner degradation. They are cunning, mischievous creatures who take delight in frightening and tormenting human villagers when they surface at night. While Princess Irene discovers an enchanting, beautiful, and gracious apparition of her great-great-grandmother (after whom she was named, and whom only Princess Irene can see) in an upper room in the castle, a young, virtuous miner boy Curdie discovers a plot by the goblins to capture the Princess to marry her to a goblin prince, thus winning back the kingdom for their kind. Irene's "Grandmother" meanwhile weaves a magic thread, which she attaches to a ring on the Princess's hand and which can lead her out of any danger. Curdie gets captured by the goblins, and Irene's ring and string lead her to rescue him from the goblins' caverns. Curdie informs the King of the goblins' plans, and the Princess, the kingdom, and the day are saved.

Within this simple plot, however, MacDonald enchants the reader into seeing a greater reality behind the ordinary. The struggle between townsfolk and goblins assumes greater and more mythical proportions than a mere political battle, as the mystical, magical grandmother beckons to the Princess and Curdie with devices (ring, string, and even her bedroom) that literally glow with enchantment. The angelic, elderly Irene explains to the Princess that "people must believe what they can, and those who believe more must not be hard upon those who believe less. I doubt you would have believed it all yourself if you hadn't seen some of it."[10] Later, when the Princess questions why Curdie can still not see Irene, she explains, "When I please I can make the lamp shine through the walls . . . not everybody can see it. It's a gift born with you. And one day I hope everybody will have it."[11] Even the magic string which saves Curdie evokes a deeper, salvific symbolism. Chesterton appropriates this in his *Father Brown* tales as Father Brown uses an invisible string to pull a thief back from evil ways, which is cited by the Christian novelist Evelyn Waugh in his *Brideshead Revisited* in which he describes God's unrelenting tug at the human soul.[12]

Chesterton credited MacDonald's inherent and other-worldly optimism for this "spiritual environment, a space and a mystical light" that was so counter to the gloomy predestination of the Calvinism of MacDonald's era, country

---

[10] George MacDonald, *The Princess and the Goblin* (New York: Penguin Books, 1996), 115.

[11] Ibid., 174.

[12] Joseph Pearce, *Catholic Literary Giants: A Field Guide to the Catholic Literary Landscape* (San Francisco: Ignatius Press, 2014), pt. 25. Digital Edition.

S. Myers   *Once a Prince or Princess*

(Scotland), and own upbringing.[13] Such a shining optimism, which Chesterton likened to the otherworldly cheer of mystical Cavaliers, Catholic saints, and even Platonists, might even come to be considered as "a rather important turning point in the history of Christendom."[14] Nineteenth century Scotland produced not just literary luminaries such as the poet Robert Burns and novelist Walter Scott, but in MacDonald it had its Francis of Assisi, who not only "saw a halo round every flower and bird" (as might even pagan poets, though without any ultimate hope), but imbued such ordinary items with a sacramental significance.[15] He not only dressed up ordinary characters as princes or princesses, Chesterton argued, but "did really believe that people were princesses and goblins and good fairies, and dressed them up as ordinary men and women."[16]

---

[13] Chesterton, *Introduction to George MacDonald and His Wife*, 304.

[14] Ibid., 305.

[15] Ibid., 306.

[16] Ibid., 303.

The Princess and Curdie: Growing into Goodness

The Princess and Curdie continues two years later, with Curdie and the Princess maturing from the thirteen- and nine-year old children they were (respectively) in the previous tale. Curdie's heroism shows throughout as he matures on a journey that resembles John Bunyan's Pilgrim in *Pilgrim's Progress*. Curdie turns down the King's offer to come travel with the royal family as they return to Gwyntystorm, a decision that impresses the King. Instead, Curdie stays with his own family and continues to work in the mines alongside his father. Chesterton discounted the sequel slightly as a story of an ordinary young man headed off to seek fortune in "a far-off fairyland," instead of a tale with the "particular purpose of making all the ordinary staircases and doors and windows into magical things;" nevertheless, in it Curdie learns to follow the path of goodness and thus find enchantment.[17] The mountain in which Curdie and his father Peter mined is declared by MacDonald as a "strange and awful thing . . . [a] beautiful terror," a convulsion of the heat and

---

[17] Chesterton, *Introduction to George MacDonald and His Wife*, 302.

heart of the earth, though people have lost their sense of them as such.[18] Curdie begins to lose his own eyes to see the world as a wonder, believing "less and less in things he had never seen," despite being a miner whose job was "to bring to light hidden things."[19] Nevertheless, the King knew that a boy who declined the offer to accompany a king for the love of his family would someday be of great use.[20] MacDonald likened Curdie's state of faith to that of humanity which is either in a state of "continuous resurrection" or "continuous dying," of knowing the truth of a thing at the moment of its encounter, or of knowing only what is between one's teeth, of coming to "believe in nothing but his dinner."[21] When Curdie finds himself hunting a snow-white pigeon merely for sport (surely an echo of Coleridge's albatross-hunting *Ancient Mariner*, written 85 years prior, in 1798), he comes to question his purpose, and finds himself following a glowing moonlight to the

---

[18] George MacDonald, *The Princess and Curdie* (New York: Penguin Books, 1994), 1.

[19] Ibid., 12.

[20] Ibid., 12,4.

[21] Ibid., 12.

castle to find the Princess Irene's ancestral, ghostly Irene. The elder Irene heals the pigeon and reminds Curdie that now that he knows the harm of such activities as reckless hunting, he needs to repent. Curdie's mother, who had seen the glowing light from Irene years ago, further reminds Curdie how the world "seems just as full of reason as it is of wonder" when she describes how the withered seeds she planted became scented, colorful flowers.[22]

Curdie grows in understanding and character as he encounters the luminary, ancestral Irene in various settings. The Mother of Light, dressed in an emerald shade, finds Peter and his father Curdie in the mines, informing them that in their poverty they have been blessed with a goodness they would not have achieved had they been rich; she also informs them that there is a royalty to their blood of which they are unaware, and she has been cultivating them for a long time. As Chesterton declared, MacDonald makes royalty of the ordinary. Curdie recognizes this in his own father, observing that "it is greed and laziness and selfishness, not hunger or weariness or cold, that

---

[22] MacDonald, *The Princess and Curdie,* 37.

take the dignity out of a man."[23] The Silver Moon, another of her twenty different names (and to know her as one name allows him to recognize her in any other, shades of Lewis's later Aslan), blesses Curdie's hands with a refining fire, a painful process which allows him to sense in men whether they are continuously dying and turning into mere sensate beasts (and even which sort of beasts they become). Of such degenerated specimens of humanity, Curdie is advised that "to such a person there is in general no insult like the truth" as "he cannot endure it, not because he is growing a beast, but because he is ceasing to be a man."[24] Curdie is then sent on a mission to find Irene and her father at the castle, though he is also given a companion, the incongruous, long, and thick-tailed, green-eyed monster with the hands of a child, named Lina.

Curdie's heroism is tested as he and Lina travel to Gwyntystorm, encountering many trials in the forest along the way. Lina proves helpful, at times even risking her life, and Curdie comes to trust his faithful but hideous-looking companion; arguably

---

[23] MacDonald, *The Princess and Curdie*, 61.

[24] Ibid., 74.

Tolkien took a cue from Lina with Frodo's companion, Gollum. Like Frodo, Curdie is at first moved with pity at such a creature, though Lina shows worth whereas Gollum displays the actions of the pale, withered shadow of a hobbit he had become. In contrast to the fallen Gollum, Luna is hinted to be a human working out her redemption. Curdie further learns to live and govern well from the King's example. The King spends the silver produced in his mines not on luxuries but to govern, defend, and pay judges to "portion out righteousness among the people" so that "when it left the king's hands it never made any but friends."[25] By contrast, when foolish townsfolk get some silver, they often "degraded it by locking it up in a chest" where "it grew diseased and was called *mammon*, and bred all sorts of quarrels."[26] Curdie's power and heroic character consists in his learning of such wisdom.

The Princess and Curdie has been criticized for the vast array of bad characters encountered by Curdie and Lina on their journey, though MacDonald must have had Bunyan's *Pilgrim's*

---

[25] MacDonald, *The Princess and Curdie*, 5.

[26] Ibid.

Progress somewhat in mind. However, balanced against preachers who summon "the dull and monotonic grind of their intellectual machines" against dishonesty then get devoured from the pulpit by giant snakes, MacDonald offers delightful encounters to instruct, such as that between Barbara and her daughter Derba as well as that of Peter's parents. Barbara and her daughter Derba offer shelter when townsfolk seek to arrest and roast, respectively, "the miner and his brute," and the innocence of little Barbara later helps expel tormenting dreams from the King's mind.[27] Curdie's parents, Peter and Joan, are likewise lauded, being described as "the happiest couple in that country" as they always understood each other "because they always meant the same thing" as they always loved what was fair and true and right better, not than anything else, but than everything else put together.[28]

The Princess and Curdie proves the worth of the heroic wisdom Curdie has learned as it concludes. Lina and Curdie eventually both end up captured in a dungeon beneath the King's

---

[27] MacDonald, *The Princess and Curdie,* 118.

[28] Ibid., 35.

castle, and manage to escape only to find that the King is being slowly poisoned by disloyal and greedy officers. Such enemies are exposed with the aid of Curdie's gift of discernment. Curdie meets the doctor poisoning the King and sees the "snake . . . plainly visible" in his face, the "evil countenance" of a man who "hated the king, and delighted in doing him harm."[29] Eventually, the King, Irene, Curdie, Lina, and her host of animal friends make war on the king's oppressors (a regiment bringing to mind the forces of Narnia arrayed against the White Witch in Lewis's *The Lion, The Witch and the Wardrobe* or in *Prince Caspian*) and defeat them. In its brief ending, Irene's celestial "Grandma" Irene reveals herself in yet another form, serving the royal company and their faithful companions, after which matters concerning the anticipated future reign of King Curdie and Queen Irene are introduced. MacDonald makes his final statement as he considers the state of the kingdom a generation after Curdie and Irene, with another king on the throne, the incessant lure of gold to be mined, and

---

[29] MacDonald, *The Princess and Curdie,* 180.

the greedy townsfolk making the fate of Gwyntytown precarious.

THE LOST PRINCESS: A DOUBLE STORY OF OVERCOMING ONESELF

The Lost Princess: A Double Story (also known as *The Wise Woman: A Parable*) continues MacDonald's focus on heroic character development, but centers on heroic princesses rather than boys who would become princes. Published in 1875 in between *The Princess and the Goblin* (1872) and *The Princess and Curdie* (1883), *The Lost Princess* is a story of two spoiled young girls learning (or not) humility. Just a few years later, MacDonald would return his focus to the moral education of young boys, as *Sir Gibbie* (1879) tells a rags to riches story about the noble youth Gibbie and his education in integrity, servanthood, and Christian obedience. *Gibbie* became popular in both Britain and America, and was revived in modern times by the recommendation of Lewis, and inspired the American writer Elizabeth Yates to applaud it with:

It moved me the way books did when, as a child, the great gates of literature began to open and first encounters with noble thoughts and utterances were unspeakably thrilling.[30]

Rosamond is the lost princess of MacDonald's (double) story, though she is not just born on the same day as Agnes, the daughter of common shepherds, she is just as spoiled. Rosamond has been overindulged by her royal parents while Agnes has been overly praised by her proud shepherding lineage; both sets of parents pay for such sins the misery wreaked on them by the young tyrants. Despite coming from such diverse backgrounds, rags and riches, each girl suffers the same exact malady, as MacDonald states of their "odd country" that it was full of boys and girls who were:

> rather too ready to think he or she was Somebody; and the worst of it was that the princess never thought of there being more than one Somebody.[31]

---

[30] Cited in "George MacDonald," *HS Treasures*, last modified August 16, 2007, accessed May 7, 2021, https://web.archive.org/web/20070816234924/http://www.hstrea sures.com/authors/george_macdonald.html Yates edited some of MacDonald's novels.

[31] George MacDonald, *The Lost Princess: A Double Tale* (United States: Start Publishing, 2012), loc. 34. Digital edition.

A mysterious Wise Woman intervenes in both cases, stealing away each girl to correct their wayward youths.

The lost princess Rosamond is the first to learn humility. She is abducted by the moral instructor, and taken to a secluded cottage in the forest and shown a magic mirror which reveals her true inner self; it is interesting to note that this was written fifteen years before Oscar Wilde's *Picture of Dorian Gray* (1890) in which a painting was used to reveal true moral character. Disgusted, terrified, and ashamed by what she sees, and with the aid of the Wise Woman's kindness, discipline and a little bit of magic, Rosamond comes to learn self-restraint, then later discovers a magic painting and steps through it to arrive on a hill near the home of Agnes. In this process, MacDonald sounds themes that will echo in the later writings of Lewis among others. In a dream, Rosamond envisions "the only shadow of a hope . . . that she might by slow degrees grow thinner and thinner, until at last she wore away to nothing at all;"[32] Lewis repeats this tune of distraction from self in *The Great Divorce* when he has MacDonald (there

---

[32] MacDonald, *The Lost Princess,* 364.

known as "the Teacher") explain the use of a stampede of unicorns parading by a self-absorbed character: "it if took her mind a moment off herself, there might, in that moment, be a chance" and "I have seen them saved so."[33]

Both Lewis and Tolkien took further cues from MacDonald on the incapacitating and dehumanizing nature of evil. The selfish princess misunderstands the Wise Woman at first, as the princess "did not in the least understand kindness" as "the wrong in her was this -- that she had led such a bad life, that she did not know a good woman when she saw her."[34] [35] Tolkien modeled evil physically in the dark and gloomy landscapes of Mordor and in the twisted, perverted beings that the once elven-orcs and once hobbit Gollum had become. Similarly Lewis models self-absorbed characters in *The Great Divorce* as insubstantial and tiny, unable to barely carry or bite into fruit, and sometimes self-imploding into nothingness. All authors hearken

---

[33] C.S. Lewis, *The Great Divorce* (New York: HarperCollins, 2000), 79.

[34] George MacDonald, *The Lost Princess*, loc. 138.

[35] Ibid., 274.

in some way back to insights such as that from Augustine that evil hardly exists on its own terms, it is simply a privation of that which is good, but MacDonald strikes the note so clearly in his fantasy literature that it reverberates clearly throughout the works of Lewis and Tolkien.[36]

Agnes spurns the lessons in humility which Rosamond embraces. Just as Rosamond escapes, the Wise Woman collects Agnes and returns to the cottage. Agnes's reaction to the revealing of her inner character is not one of humility and repentance but denial, and she resolves to simply conceal her conceit while appearing outwardly obedient. Agnes also discovers the magic portrait gallery and steps through a painting to find herself at the palace where Rosamond's parents search for their missing daughter. Agnes finds work in the royal kitchen, where she seeks attention by hinting that she can find the lost princess; it works, and soon the King and Queen send for her. Meanwhile, Agnes's parents search for their lost daughter, only to find Rosamond, whom they nurse back to health and decide to keep in place of Agnes. Rosamond makes a

---

[36] Augustine, *Confessions*, Book VII.

sincere effort at reformation, but returns to her selfish, spoiled nature, and is asked to leave. Rosamond then searches for the Wise Woman's cottage, dedicated to returning to her previous albeit brief state of humility, and becomes lost though the Wise woman rescues her. After failing several trials by her instructor's magic, Rosamond looks into the magic mirror once more, only to find that the mirror is in fact the Wise Woman's eyes, and that she has merely seen how beautiful the Wise Woman believed Rosamond could become. The Wise Woman then returns Rosamond home, through the magical gallery. Rosamond demonstrates the never-ending struggle of heroes, as temptations always arise to test her "powers," the humility that she has learned.

Agnes and Rosamond conclude the tale by showing the true worth of humility. Back at the palace Rosamond and Agnes finally meet, though they (and their parents) make a portrait of perfect contrasts. Agnes's parents are accused of kidnapping Rosamond, but when Rosamond dashes into the courtroom to defend them, she is so transformed that her own parents do not recognize her. The Wise Woman explains to

Rosamond's parents that they are so superficial that they cannot recognize goodness when it is standing in front of their very eyes. The Wise Woman then curses them with blindness until they reform their ways, and Rosamond offers to care for them in the meanwhile. Agnes is then returned to her parents by the Wise Woman, declaring that since they made Agnes into what she is, Agnes will now be their punishment. The father shows true repentance, begging the Wise Woman to teach him; she agrees, proceeding to take him to her cottage, but not before she promises Rosamond to always be nearby should she need her moral tutor. Humble Rosamond and hubristic Agnes, along with their parents, prove that heroic powers are at their best when heroes think the least of themselves.

CONCLUSION: LESSONS FOR PRINCESSES. AND PRINCESS

The moral struggle found in *The Lost Princess* resonates with the theme of courage found throughout MacDonald's other *Princess* tales as well as throughout this *AUJ* issue devoted to superheroes. Agnes might appear courageous in her trials but it was only a fearlessness born of ignorance and "calm assured self-satisfaction," while for Rosamund, her endurance through trials was courage in the face of fear, as MacDonald states that "the man who will do his work in spite of his fear is a man of true courage."[37] Similarly, MacDonald uses Agnes and Rosamond to compare the effects of partial submission to one's work, or duty, as Agnes illustrates how "to do one's duty will make any pone conceited who only does it sometimes" whereas Rosamond illustrates how "until our duty becomes to us as common as breathing, we are poor creatures;" Superheroes are so bound by duty as to not even notice their own super-sized status, as their powers are meant to serve rather than self-glorify.[38]

Taken all together, MacDonald's *Princess* tales illustrate the moral courage required at each step of an ordinary life to achieve the status of a moral superhero. *The Princess and the Goblin* continues the program of MacDonald's most famous fantasy, *Phantastes*, in showing that life's seemingly ordinary struggles are anything but ordinary, but a colossal battle between glorious

---

[37] George MacDonald, *The Lost Princess,* loc. 664.

[38] Ibid., loc. 731.

good and pernicious evil. *The Princess and Curdie* continues the story, fleshing out the various forms in which that battle is met in the course of life's journeys. Finally, *The Lost Princess: A Double Tale* highlights the courage required in the continuing struggle against the self, as well as the resources of a wise guide (the Wise Woman) in helping us along the way.

Superheroes, Saviors, and C.S. Lewis

James M. Swayze on Epic, Myth, and
Human Longings

Introduction

In a time of great scientific and technical
achievement, when humanity seems to revel in a
self-praise approaching hubris, how can it be that
fictional superheroes occupy such an expansive
position in the shared cultural psyche? What does
our modern-day obsession with these spandex-
clad *über-menschen* say about us? In this paper,
we will attempt to shed light on this cultural
phenomenon by examining C.S. Lewis's ideas of
imagination and story, myth and epic as well as
his critique of modernism and postmodernism.

Imagination

In Lewis's essay "Bluspels and Flalansferes", he
argues that while facts about the universe in
which we live are obtained via human reason --
proposition, deduction, and syllogism -- the way
we make *sense* of this data is via the process of

"stitching together" data into images. "Reason is the natural organ of truth," Lewis tells us, but "imagination is the organ of meaning."[1] We only grasp the meaning of something, understand it, when we are able to form images in our minds. It is the way we are "wired."

STORY AND EPIC

Where imagination is a necessary precondition of meaning, a transformation of mere facts or data, *story* consists of an ordering of images into a narrative whole. Story is how we make sense of the world. We each have one.

Epic, the highest form of story, consists of grand, sweeping accounts, stages upon which heroes and superheroes play. The form resides at the very foundation of a culture and is a primary means by which a people make sense of the world and their place in it. Our post-Christian sensibilities revolt against the very idea of a grand, sweeping story, which in our soul-poverty we have replaced with the notion that life is but an

---

[1] C.S. Lewis, "Bluspels and Flalansferes" from *Selected Literary Essays* (Cambridge, Cambridge University Press, 2015), 265.

accident -- and humans are animals at best, a sort of virus at worst.

But is mere *accident,* a materialist world in which reality is little more than billiard balls colliding with other billiard balls and human thoughts are but atoms banging about in skulls, an accurate reflection of reality? If *story* is how we make sense of our world, could it be that the Christian account of the nature of things is actually better than the ascendant sordid and cynical modern worldview? Christian author John Eldredge tells us that:

> . . . when we were born, we were born into the midst of a great story begun before the dawn of time. A story of adventure, of risk and loss, heroism . . . and betrayal. A story where good is warring against evil, danger lurks around every corner, and glorious deeds wait to be done. Think of all those stories you've ever loved--there's a reason they stirred your heart. They've been trying to tell you about the true Epic ever since you were young. . . . There is a larger story. And you have a crucial role to play.[2]

---

[2] John Eldredge, "The Story You Fell Into," *Wild at Heart,* accessed May 8, 2021. https://wildatheart.org/story/larger-story/story-you-fell-into.

MYTH

Another form of story is myth. Where epic is broad and monumental, myth -- while similarly set at the conjunction of divine and human worlds -- consists of a single episode, one of deep, often enormously profound, import. Myth is a brief story, one made of "images that [strike] roots far below the surface of [one's] mind."[3]

In common parlance, myth means that which is false. Lewis, however, tells us that the standard myth, while factually untrue, is a pointer to deeper truth. It is something "extra-literary," something "which would equally delight and nourish if it had reached . . . by some medium which involved no words at all."[4] Myth is story that strikes deeply.

HEROES AND SUPERHEROES

The success of Patty Jenkins's Wonder Woman, depicting warring Olympians and Amazons, continues to stoke moviegoer interest in Greek mythology. . . . But is Greek myth simply a favoured and enduring wellspring for heroic sagas full of

---

[3] C.S. Lewis, *An Experiment in Criticism* (Cambridge, Cambridge University Press, 2013), 49.

[4] Lewis, *An Experiment in Criticism,* 43.

supermen and monsters or are there deeper forces at play? [5]

Epics are the stages upon which heroes play. And a hero is a *good* person, the best, strongest, smartest -- larger than life yet fully human (though often of divine descent) -- one who battles evil on our behalf. To be a hero is to be a rescuer or conqueror. Sometimes heroes are fully human but simply endowed with exemplary ability; basketball "god" Michael Jordan comes to mind. But, throughout time, our heroes have descended from divinity, a result of interrelations between god and man.

The key is this: Heroes are *one of us*; they're on *our team*. And nine times out of ten (if not ten times out of ten), they've come to unequivocally dominate, to impose their will with physical force, to rescue the village, the city, the region, the country, or the world from evil forces that have come to destroy all that is good and right. One thinks not only of Western heroes Aeneas,

---

[5]Paul Salmond, "Journeys to the Underworld: From Ancient Greece to Hollywood, " *Ancient Origins,* accessed May 8, 2021 www.ancient-origins.net/news-history-archaeology/journeys-underworld-ancient-greece-holywood-008880.

Achilles, or Beowulf, but also non-Western figures such as the Indian hero Rama or the Samurai of Japan.

What then is a *super*-hero? By definition, they are *a hero with more*. Yes, they're our guy (or gal). Yes, they are the strongest, the smartest, the best of the best. Yes, they fight evil, that which threatens our way, our families. But the "more" consists not in mere superior strength or ability, but super-ability, super-strength; in short, super-human qualities.

Where Achilles is a hero of the Trojan War and Michael Jordan is a hero of the basketball court who plays the game *as if he could fly*, Superman actually *can* fly. But where Jordan is real, Superman is not. Having abandoned the supernaturally-touched worlds in which god and man used to play, our superheroes are gods come to earth.

CHRIST AND SUPERHEROES

Enter the figure of Christ. Jewish messianic, heroic expectations generally held (and still hold) that Messiah would come to forever rescue Israel from her earthly overlords. He certainly would not do something anti-heroic like being utterly, completely, and finally humiliated by being publicly flogged, spit upon, and nailed to a cross, executed by the very powers whom he's come to conquer!

Jesus is a just, courageous, noble, rescuing figure, both human and divine, and with superhuman powers. He did come on the scene where dark powers were strongly evident, and with the purpose of setting the world to rights. But, unlike the superhero, he very strongly eschewed violence.

THE RECENT REJECTION OF CHRISTIAN ORTHODOXY

Modernism rejects such nonsense. Myth is fine and well, as long as it's kept in its place and one does not get the ridiculous notion that mythic figures could possibly exist in reality.[6] Lewis, a thoroughgoing orthodox Christian, was an able critic of Enlightenment and post-Enlightenment secularism.

Though the roots of Christendom are deep, even to this day, we have been engaged in a

---

[6] It is an interesting question as to the degree to which cultures over time believed in the literal existence of their heroes. For instance, did the Roman believe that Romulus and Remus were actual human beings raised by wolves? One would guess not.

program that rejects the core assumptions of the faith, not least the idea of the Fall. We moderns have held that people are at their core good beings who have simply been corrupted by their environments. Where Christianity says that people are quite literally a damned mess, we now believe that people are blank slates. These are not new ideas, the *tabula rasa* and the noble savage. Variations of such arguments were put forward by Aristotle in *De Anima*. But the idea found new favor with Enlightenment-era rationalist thinkers such as Locke and Rousseau.[7]

In the late 19th and early 20th centuries, the assault on Christianity continued with Marx, Freud, and Nietzche arguing that rather than being creations *of* God, God is *our* creation. In *Das Kapital*, Marx gave us the notion that good and evil are not part of the nature of a created order but rather a mere reflection of the values of whichever group happens to possess the most political power. To Freud, God is mere wish fulfillment.[8] And Nietzche, more than any other

---

[7] See Locke's "An Essay Concerning Human Understanding" and Rousseau's *Emile*.

[8] See Freud's *The Future of an Illusion*.

modern thinker grasping the implications of the seemingly-newfound realization that God is but a human invention, declared – heroically, but with reluctance and regret -- that God is dead and life is abysmal.

Another key modern idea is reductionism. Freud informed us that we've built imaginary beings such as God as a defense against what is really a cold, hard world. Love is only sex, he tells us, friendship only a sublimated means by which we get what we really want. Following that theme, we now know that Christ is only (there's the key reductionist word, "only") yet another retelling of age-old myths.

Let's take the story of Jesus's descent into Hell. Many cultures, perhaps most, tell the same story. For example, "to the Greeks, the underworld journey was an ideal vehicle for the hero to display his exceptional qualities, often involving the rescue of a soul trapped there."[9] So, like Jesus, both Odysseus and Aeneas journey to the underworld and return. And since the Greek stories are older, the Christian account must be *only* a copy, a derivative retelling of the same

---

[9] Salmond, "Journeys to the Underworld."

fictional story that has been told since time immemorial.

In *The Abolition of Man*, Lewis turns the reductionist idea on its head by showing us that if the Christian account of the world is true, if God is truly the author of all reality, it is no surprise that earlier cultures would tell such stories. Lewis held that all human societies have at least some truth about them and are not to be rejected outright. But Christianity is God's ultimate revelation about the true nature of the world and our place in it. Where paganism reflected bits and pieces of truth, to Lewis, "Christianity fulfilled paganism."[10]

CONCLUSION

Every human has a story, a way of making sense of their place in the world. Every culture has their larger story. We moderns – in our arrogance believing that, of all peoples who ever lived, we have the best grasp of the nature of reality -- have since the Enlightenment expended great effort to attempt to show that life is but an accident, the universe but a random collocation of elements.

---

[10] Roger Lancelyn Green, *C.S. Lewis: A Biography* (New York, Harcourt Publishing, 1974), 274.

But try as we might, we cannot escape the allure of epic and myth, hero and superhero. It is the way we are wired.

We can, however, escape the present. We *were* born into a real-life grand, sweeping epic. Our superheroes, whether Superman or Wonder Woman, the Green Lantern or Captain America, are but recent instances of the age-old desire for a savior, one who will right all wrongs and wipe away every tear.

THE POWER OF WEAKNESS

Jesse Baker on Questions of Violence

I love the large story arc the Marvel universe has gradually unfolded over the last ten years or so. Not every movie is perfect by any stretch, but the way they have woven the various stories together has been captivating. One drawback to these otherwise great movies is their violence. To some degree the violence makes sense, as many of the movies revolve around power struggles. One person has power (whether a particular title or ability) and another person wants it, and is willing to do whatever necessary to get it. Once the villain gets the power, it makes sense that another strong man or woman must be there to stand in the way. For the safety of all involved the threat must be eliminated. While I do enjoy these movies, I have wondered if the violence and power struggles are perhaps unintentionally glorified since these elements are so often repeated in Marvel's various movies. Personally, I wonder if my enjoyment of these violent movies is somehow an indictment on my faith. Should I just leave them alone and stick with more wholesome movies like *God's Not Dead* or *Fireproof*? Or is there a deeper way these movies actually align with our Christian faith?

Near the beginning of 2020, I was leading a Bible study on Revelation while I was re-watching all the Marvel movies I had access to. Revelation, as any reader of it will immediately recognize, is a pretty violent book in its own right. Since so much of the book is symbolic and the symbols are so odd and confusing, the violence is one of the few things that seems understandable. In that most recent reading of Revelation, however, something became clear to me. Never were those who are faithful to Jesus the initiators of violence. On the other hand, they experience it. Any violence enacted on those who oppose Jesus and his kingdom comes directly from God. John, no doubt, was familiar with the book of Deuteronomy where God speaks through Moses and says, "Vengeance is mine."[1] This is consistent throughout Revelation. Even the great battle of Armageddon, often elevated in importance and

---

[1] Deuteronomy 32:35 (NRSV).

emphasized by certain strands within the church, ultimately comes across as a surprising letdown for violence lovers as no actual battle takes place. Everyone shows up and then God takes care of his enemies rather quickly.[2] John is most certainly trying to drive home the idea that any violence the world has to offer is ultimately no opposition to God and, by extension, to God's people.

The reason violence is ultimately so weak in Revelation is stated near the beginning of the book. Shortly after John is escorted into the heavenly temple, he is told about someone described as the "Lion of the tribe of Judah, the Root of David, [who] has conquered."[3] When John sees this person, however, the description is radically different: "Then I saw. . . a Lamb standing as if it had been slaughtered."[4] The hearing and the seeing reveal a combined picture that points to Revelation's fuller reality. All violence, all evil,

---

[2] Revelation 16:12-16; 19:17-21 (NRSV). Michael J. Gorman, *Reading Revelation Responsibly* (Eugene, OR: Cascade Books, 2011), 142. Gorman notes that some commentators think the first mention of the Battle at Megiddo actually takes place in the Revelation narrative in 19:17-21. However one looks at the battle, it is, in the end, anticlimactic.

[3] Revelation 5:5 (NRSV).

[4] Revelation 5:6 (NRSV).

and death itself have been overcome and conquered by one who was made weak and was killed. Later in Revelation Jesus shows up on a white horse riding into battle; but, before the battle starts John notes that his robe is already "dipped in blood."[5] In other words, the victory in the battle is already certain — even accomplished! — because of the death he previously endured. The *might* that is on display in Revelation is a result of the *weakness* of the Lamb. Victory comes through Jesus' sacrificial death.

This inversion of ideas (strength in weakness) gave me a new lens with which to view the Marvel movies. While violence is inescapably a big part of them, there is always a moment when the characters realize that strength and fighting will not actually win the day. Iron Man tells Pepper Potts to blow up the facility, putting himself in harm's way, in order to take out his nemesis and protect others.[6] Captain America, in order to save

---

[5] Revelation 19:13 (NRSV).

[6] *Iron Man*, directed by Jon Favreau, (Marvel Studios, 2008), accessed through https://www.disneyplus.com.

millions, crashes the aircraft he is flying in.[7] Thor literally has a death and resurrection scene in his origin movie after offering his own life that others might be spared the wrath of his brother's anger.[8] Tony Stark snaps his finger at the end of *Endgame* to take out Thanos and his army, resulting in his own death.[9]

More often than not, the superheroes come to the conclusion that weakness is the path to victory as a last resort. Obviously, for Jesus it was the first and only option. While these movies do not perfectly align with the Christian story, when I re-watch the Marvel movies through the lens of Revelation, I realize there is something deeper drawing me in. One reason these stories have such an amazing pull on me is that they are tapping in to a deeper narrative, not just an imaginative tale — but a real one, where the most powerful person became weakest and suffered

---

[7] *Captain America: The First Avenger*, directed by Joe Johnson, (Marvel Studios, 2011), accessed through https://www.disneyplus.com.

[8] *Thor*, directed by Kenneth Branagh, (Marvel Studios, 2011), accessed through https://www.disneyplus.com.

[9] *Avengers: Endgame*, directed by Anthony Russo and Joe Russo, (Marvel Studios, 2019), accessed through https://www.disneyplus.com.

death so that death itself would be ultimately destroyed. The superhero movies resonate with Jesus's story once those heroes learn they do their best work when they renounce their power for the sake of others. Therefore, the heart of these movies lies not in the violence they show, but in the beauty of the sacrifices made and weaknesses displayed. In that way they even become a means for introducing others to the world's True Lover, and the one who showed us, not on screen but in history, that "No one has greater love than this, to lay down one's life for one's friends."[10]

---

[10] John 15:13 (NRSV).

Humility Contra Pride as Represented in *Thor* (2011)

John P. Tuttle on the Superiority of Virtue

Lately, there has been a lot of talk about the real-life heroes of our day and age, those who serve and care for others, offering even the smallest charitable acts. If being a hero means being selfless, then – to some extent – it follows that such people may be heralded as heroes.

In the realm of the fantastic, "superheroes" are not treated nor expected to be taken as ordinary individuals. Their difference manifests itself most often through unique physical characteristics and abilities which are not inherent to human beings.

Throughout comics and films, superheroes come in an array of forms including aliens and non-human entities, such as Groot from Marvel's *Guardians of the Galaxy*. It is fantastic characters like these that tend to possess an element of the superhuman.

A superhero is frequently introduced into his or her storyline through the background of mourner, underdog, or penitent. The mourner grapples with loss and grief. The underdog finds a calling, is given a chance, and takes the initiative to become better. The penitent is called to acknowledge the defect of past actions and, moving forward, strive to be better.

Chris Hemsworth's titular character in the Marvel Cinematic Universe's *Thor* (2011) is exemplary of the last of these character dispositions. Much to his agitation, Thor is thrust into the normative human condition, no longer being able to wield the tremendous power of his hammer, Mjolnir. Descending from the heights of his royal home in Asgard, Thor enters into the human condition. His extraordinary strength is gone; he finds himself having a physical weakness comparable to that of any other human being. In so many ways, he shares in the helplessness of the people of Earth, thus being taught a lesson in humility.

Humility, as understood through the lens of Christianity, is inseparable from a virtuous life. It goes hand in hand with charity, docility, obedience, and other virtues.

A general definition of *humility* is designated as that "supernatural virtue by which one attains the correct perception of one's relationship with God ... The attitude of humility is: 'I am good only because of God's mercy.' Humility counters pride and seeks to serve God and others, as Mary did."[1] The Virgin Mary's example of humbly accepting the will of God stands in stark contrast with the long line of disobedience, disregard, and grumblings of God's people in the Old Testament. With Mary's "yes," a new age is able to be ushered in, and through her collaboration with God, she was able not only to serve Him, but the whole of humanity. A crucial aspect of humility then is helping others rather than looking to one's own self-interests, while pride seeks the opposite of this.

Not of his own accord, Thor is temporarily cast down into a trial which he finds bothersome, even seemingly hopeless at times. The scenario puts him out of his element, jettisoned from the fullness of his glory by his father Odin. Moreover, his relationship with his father is damaged by his

---

1 Rev. Peter M.J. Stravinskas, ed., *Our Sunday Visitor's Catholic Dictionary* (Huntington, IN: Our   Sunday Visitor, Inc., 1993), 257.

disobedience. In a sense, Odin recognizes the importance of humility in the role of leadership. If Thor is going to be a superhero – not to mention a king – he must adhere to the "supernatural virtue" of humility.

In the script for *Thor*, though the line is inaudible, Odin tells his first-born son at the coronation ceremony, "Responsibility, duty, honor: these are not merely virtues to which we must aspire. They are essential to every soldier, to every king."[2]

This showcases just how important virtue is to the role of a just ruler. The king must not be lacking in his duties. As with many Christian virtues, humility is a common link between the marks of authentic leadership that Odin listed. True humility instills a proactive instinct toward serving others as well as a proper sense of self-respect. For a benevolent leader in the public sphere, these are crucial marks of character, ones which Thor needs to uphold.

From the earliest stages of the film, Loki, a figure of sorcery and deception (who is the

---

2 Ashley Miller, Zack Stentz, and Don Payne, "THOR," *Script Slug*, accessed April 10, 2021, https://www.scriptslug.com/assets/uploads/scripts/thor-2011.pdf.

adopted son of Odin) plays the people around him like pawns, servile pieces in a scheme propelled by his own twisted contrivances. He whispers sweet, seductive poison to Thor, confirming his brother's inclinations, dissuading him from the will of their father. Notice that once pride becomes a point of control, deception is close to follow. Thor, having taken an oath to cast aside selfish ambition and subsequently disobeying his father's commandment of non-retaliation, is banished. While remaining physically robust, he faces the consequences of being stripped of his immortality, the supernatural capabilities bestowed upon him, and his honorary decorations. Most dramatically, however, his hammer Mjolnir is no longer in his control. During much of the course of the film, Thor's newfound frailty is pushed to its limit as he repeatedly falls victim to being pummeled by vehicles, wounded by weapons, and found susceptible to the strength of other mortals. His trip to Earth is a truly humiliating one.

As the plot progresses, Thor interacts more with humans, all the while Loki connives and seeks to supplant the power of Odin and Thor. He would betray his foster father and, at his own hands, murdered Laufey, king of the Frost Giants and Loki's biological father. His prideful self-interest spurs him on toward the fringes of madness. Pride not only leads to deception of oneself and others, but it also reaps anger.

Throughout the film, Loki confronts Thor, letting his deceptions fall upon his brother's ears. Eventually, he sends a metallic automaton to Earth to combat his brother in order to eliminate him as a contender for the throne. It is at this point of the film that Thor starts to clearly display elements of humility. Steering away from personal safety, Thor speaks to Loki through the medium provided by the automaton, telling him that such violence should be unleashed not on the innocent bystanders but only upon himself.

Unrelenting, Loki's mechanical minion inflicts tremendous injury on Thor to the point that his body falls motionless to the ground and stirs neither eye nor limb. In this moment of apparent defeat, having given perhaps the ultimate self-sacrifice, Thor's hammer returns to him. He has become worthy to grasp and wield it once more. Through humility, this Asgardian becomes victorious.

This first installment in Thor's side-saga of films not only displays the need and benefits of humility. But it also shows the dangerous drive of the ego and of self-interest through pride. As humbled as Thor has become by the climax of the movie, so too have Loki's grief and pangs for dominance escalated to the extreme. Like Romulus and Remus, whose monumental relationship was undermined by jealousies, ambition, and petty mockery, Thor and Loki are contrasted against one another. In the end, there is no soothing Loki's prideful lust for power.

In an allegorical sense, Hemsworth's Thor could be taken as a Christ figure. He descends from on high, is meant to be a king, lives in a humbled state, lays down his life to save many, and overcomes one of the gravest of mortal obstacles. Apart from being anything but fantastic, Christ's relationship with humanity differs from Thor's since He remains humble, and yet His majesty, while sometimes hidden, remains constant. Nevertheless, Thor shares this example of Christ – as we are all called to share in. The purpose is not to be served, but to serve.

In *Miracles*, the acclaimed writer and professor C.S. Lewis says, "To be high or central means to abdicate continually: to be low means to be raised: all good masters are servants: God washes the feet of men."[3]

The Son of Man came to serve. His example of poverty and servitude lays a foundation for Christians. He has given His followers an image of humility through selflessness and service. Being a leader now entails being a servant.

At one point, when Thor confronts his brother directly upon his return to Asgard, Loki tries once more to sway Thor's mindset away from mercy. Loki intends to destroy Jotenheim, the world of the Frost Giants, but Thor – who had earlier instigated harsh retaliation against them – advocates for mercy. He fights against Loki, who has now tossed out any idea of the wellbeing of others. He does not see beyond his own will and gain, whereas Thor has become the opposite to this. Even while Loki is in the act of appealing to his brother's emotive inclinations, the noble hammer-wielder chooses to sacrifice his own

---

[3] Patricia S. Klein, ed., *A Year with C.S. Lewis: Daily Readings from His Classic Works* (New   York: HarperCollins Publishers, 2003), 150.

desires for the superior good. Thor destroys the portal which would give Loki the ability to obliterate the world of Jotenheim. This salvific action simultaneously includes the possibility of never again seeing the love of his life. Thor knows this and chooses to sacrifice his own interests for the good of others. Regardless of the pain this may cause him, he decides to thwart Loki's plans of genocide.

In the end, Thor acknowledges in the presence of his father that he still has a great deal to learn. No longer does he think that he will automatically be some great ruler. He sees the role of a leader as a servant of the people, not a figure who lets himself be driven wherever his selfish desires take him. The self-interested, impulsive character he had at the beginning of the story has been subdued. The lesson of Odin shows that it is not royal blood that denotes kingship but depth of virtue.

Thus, *Thor* presents two paths in the moral life, attached to which are the consequences of each. The fruit of pride is injury to oneself and others, that of humility – service, charity, and due recognition. To be a good warrior, a good king, a good *superhero*, Thor had to learn humility. As the penitent sinner, he acknowledges the erroneous path on which he had pursued vainglorious ends. Having learned the importance of virtue, of obedience and dedication, Thor is equipped to become a good and just leader.

Like the sons of Odin, we have two paths to choose from. The general criteria for being a worthy superhero are identical to those of being an ordinary hero: not well-toned muscles, but virtues well-gained.

Just a Sidekick?

Annie Nardone on the Importance of Support

And though a man might prevail against one who is alone, two will withstand him - a threefold cord is not quickly broken.

— Ecclesiastes 4:12 (ESV)

When we think about heroic characters like Batman, Green Lantern, and Harry Potter, they are seldom the stories of loners. Each superhero has an assistant, friend, organized helper, added muscle — a sidekick. The term sidekick leaves the immediate impression of an undistinguished 'also-ran' character, not nearly as important as the lead. Upon closer examination, the steadfast partner-in-crime is absolutely key to the plot and the playing out of the tale, occupying a necessary role in balancing out the eccentricities of the lead hero.

Batman had Alfred as his quiet and supportive helper who managed the details at home, never once missing the opportunity to offer a well-timed piece of advice. Sherlock Holmes had Watson, also a steadying personality to bring Sherlock's larger-than-life personality back down to earth. Watson is a humanizing force in the Holmes mysteries, jotting notes, mentioning possible connections, or patiently listening to Sherlock's theories and ramblings. But there is more to each pair than what we first observe. There is brain to balance out the brawn, a calm presence to soothe the stormy mind, and even a little added muscle to get the heroic job done.

What brings about the first meeting of the two? C.S. Lewis suggests that "friendship arises out of a mere Companionship when two or more of the companions discover that they have in common some insight or interest or even taste which the others do not share and which, till that moment, each believed to be his own unique treasure (or burden)."[1] The hero feels the burden of righting a wrong, saving the weak, or rescuing society. The sidekick joins the fray. They are both, as Lewis describes, "about something" together, and this is the basis of friendship.

---

[1] C.S. Lewis, *The Four Loves* (New York: Harcourt, 1988), 65.

Teamwork and a common vision for setting things right is the very core of this relationship, a friendship between the two that is quite like what Lewis wrote about in his book, *The Four Loves*. Lewis describes that friendship "is essentially between individuals; the moment two men are friends they have in some degree drawn apart together from the herd."[2] Superheroes and their sidekicks are definitely set apart from the herd; honestly, they are in the business of saving the herd from itself.

---

[2] Lewis, *The Four Loves*, 58.

Two are Better Than One

Adventure calls for a loyal sidekick
Bestowed with the most inclusive of names.
Backup to heroes whom the fates may pick.

Stout-hearted champion of noble aims,
Destiny of service, at times a saving grace.
Equal in import, cohort in the game.

Stalwart companion, but not to replace.
The vision is grander than top billing.
A shared goal, adding courage to the race.

For rescue and redemption, both winning,
As two merged shadows, essential in league.
Zeal for justice, defense in the living.

To lift up his fellow, a cord not weak,
Steadfastly together, mercy they seek.

Planets, Poetry, and the Power of Myth in Halo and Destiny

Seth Myers on the Apologetic Power of Video Games

Courage is not simply one of the virtues, but the form of every virtue at the testing point . . . A chastity or honesty, or mercy, which yields to danger will be chaste or honest or merciful only on conditions. Pilate was merciful till it became risky.[1]

– C.S. Lewis, The Screwtape Letters #29

"*What became Fact was a Myth [and] carries with it into the world of Fact all the properties of a Myth . . . We must not be ashamed of the mythical radiance resting on our theology . . . If God chooses to be mythopoeic -- and is not the sky itself a Myth -- shall we refuse to be mythopathic? For this is the perfect marriage of heaven*

---

[1] C.S. Lewis, *The Screwtape Letters* (New York: HarperCollins, 2000), 161.

and earth: Perfect Myth and Perfect Fact."[2]

- C.S. Lewis, Myth Became Fact

The stories of *Halo* and its sequel series *Destiny* hinge on embattled, heroic combatants discovering hidden, secret resources from Earth's early and mysterious origin to aid them in their struggle to save humanity. That knowledge of our origins can provide the key to our fate and even our strength recurs in various superhero tales, such as that of *Superman*. Even before the COVID virus arrived in early 2020, the video game market had come to dwarf the box office receipts of the film industry, as in 2019 gaming revenues in the US alone garnered $60.59 compared to the $11.4 billion of box office receipts in North America's theaters (and $42.5 billion worldwide).[3] [4] Gaming

---

[2] C.S. Lewis, "Myth Became Fact" in *God in the Dock* (Grand Rapids: Eerdmans. 2001), 67.

[3] "Market Size of the Video Game Industry in the United States from 2010 to 2020," *Statista*, accessed May 7, 2021, www.statista.com/statistics/246892/value-of-the-video-game-market-in-the-us/

[4] Pamela McClintock, "Global Box Office Revenue Hit Record $42.5 B Despite 4 Percent Dip in U.S." *Billboard*, last modified January 11, 2020, accessed May 7, 2021,

has come a long way since the days of *Checkers,*
Nine Men's Morris, Chess, Mr. Who, Mousetrap,
Candyland, The Game of Life, Dungeons and
Dragons, Made for Trade, Monopoly, Risk,
Civilization the board game, and *Axis and Allies;*
real-time choices, multiplayer online platforms,
realistic graphics, and interactive character and
story arcs (role playing) in which the gamer
participates in a predefined but flexible story
narrative are now the norm. Were the games a
book or movie, the gamer could declare along
with Pee Wee Herman, "I don't need to see the
movie, Dottie, I lived it."[5] Prompted by the poetic
interpretation of the *Halo* series by Cambridge
poet and chaplain Malcolm Guite, integrated with
music from the games' soundtrack artist Marty
O'Donnell, we look at the deeper mythology
found, for those with eyes to see, in the *Halo -*
Destiny.game series.

The *Destiny* video series, first released in 2014
by Activision then in 2019 by its developer Bungie,

---

www.billboard.com/articles/news/8547827/2019-global-box-office-revenue-hit-record-425b-despite-4-percent-dip-in-us.

[5] *Pee Wee's Big Adventure,* directed by Tim Burton (Warner Brothers, 1985).

is a continuation of the critically acclaimed *Halo* series (with five releases since 2001, and *Halo Infinite* due out in Fall 2021). *Destiny* continues the *Halo* story, an interstellar war (genocidal holy war, to be specific, begun in the year 2525) between humans and an alien religious order (the Covenant) bent on humanity's destruction. The Covenant relies on giant ring-shaped "Halo" structures, left by the ancient race of Forerunners and serving as weapons to suppress a parasite Flood which spread throughout the galaxy. When humans discover them, they believe them to be portals for achieving transcendence. Technologically outgunned, outmanned, outnumbered, and out-planned human Spartan warriors fight valiantly for the survival of humanity against the Covenant, which eventually falls under its own hypocrisies and comes to the aid of the humans, though tensions continue between the new race of Spartans created by the United Nations Space Command (UNSC) and its colonists.

Destiny continues the story as the player is cast in the role of a Guardian, tasked to defend the last safe city on Earth against alien attackers, wielding a power named Light in its defense.

Guardians travel to other planets to destroy alien threats and are also tasked with finding a celestial being, the Traveler. A celestial sphere whose nature is unknown, the Traveler was first discovered on Mars and is responsible for allowing interplanetary travel. After sacrificing itself defending earth, it hovers dormant above earth, allowing The City to be built under the shadow of its protection against threats from the Darkness.[6]

Guite, in league with Marty O'Donnell, composer for the *Halo* and *Destiny* soundtracks, composed a set of paired poems for *Destiny*, illustrating the characteristics which have historically been associated with the planets.[7] For instance, Jupiter was considered by Ancients and Medievals as the king of the planets owing to its lion-scale size, a role borne out by the later astronomical observation that it protects life on earth from a stream of asteroids. Other celestial citizens of significance include the golden light-

[6] "The Traveler," *Destiny Wiki*. accessed May 7, 2021, www.destiny.fandom.com/wiki/The_Traveler.

[7] Malcolm Guite, "The Music of the Spheres: a poetic adventure resumes," *Malcolm Guite*, February 23, 2019, accessed May 7, 2021, www.malcolmguite.wordpress.com/tag/destiny/.

giving Sun, the silver light-reflecting Moon, swift and erratic Mercury (owing to its short circuit around the Sun) associated with commerce and communication, the war-like red planet of Mars, the life-nurturing and feminine Venus, and Saturn, which came to represent wisdom as well as suffering. That C.S. Lewis used the imagery and associated meaning of each planet to illustrate his *Chronicles of Narnia* fantasy series is the claim of Oxford University's Michael Ward, as elaborated in *Planet Narnia: The Seven Heavens in the Imagination of C.S. Lewis* and *The Narnia Code*.[8] [9] Guite's paired poems for each of these seven cosmic orbs, one for the virtuous, redeemed version of the planet's characteristic qualities, and one for it in its fallen state, as a vice, were dedicated to Ward in the compilation *Seven Heavens, Seven Hells: A Sequence for the Spheres* found in Guite's collection of poems *After Prayer*

---

[8] Michael Ward, *Planet Narnia: The Seven Heavens in the Imagination of C.S. Lewis* (Oxford: Oxford University Press, 2008). This is Ward's doctoral dissertation.

[9] Michael Ward, *The Narnia Code* (Cambridge: Tyndale House, 2010). At 224 pages, still a substantial work, but oriented for a popular audience.

(2019).[10] Each of the poems are also set to music from the Destiny soundtrack and read by Guite at his site.[11] Guite's deep, rich, sonorous, and sinewy voice is worth the effort to hear, one is reminded of the gathering of the minstrel of Gondor who sings of Frodo of the Nine Fingers and the Ring of Doom whose "clear voice . . . rose like silver and gold, and all men are hushed" until "hearts, wounded with sweet words, overflowed, and their joy was like swords, and they passed in thought out to regions where pain and delight flow together and tears are the very wine of blessedness."[12]

Humanity's struggle against alien misrule, extermination in fact, is deftly illustrated by Guite's lyrics. The *Jupiter II* poem illustrates how bad kings misuse and devour their subjects:

---

[10] Malcolm Guite, *After Prayer: New sonnets and other poems* (Norwich: Canterbury Press, 2019).

[11] Malcolm Guite, *The Music of the Spheres: a poetic adventure resumes,* last modified February 23, 2019. Accessed May 7, 2021, www.malcolmguite.wordpress.com/tag/destiny/.

[12] J.R.R. Tolkien," *Return of the King* (NewYork: Ballantine, 2001), Book V, Ch. 4, "The Field of Cormallen," 250.

Come fill the cup, whether you will or no,
For the Great Leader, you will drink it up.
His grateful people must put on a show . . .

Or you and yours will suffer. One false step
And someone disappears. They say below
His banquet hall the tortured cry for help.[13]

By contrast, the rule they truly desire is displayed in Guite's virtuous *Jupiter*:

Come fill the cup and let the fountain flow
Your king has come! There is a feast to
*   keep*
With kindled eyes and faces all aglow.[14]

Servants to such a king find themselves ennobled, just as Lewis claimed in *The Screwtape Letters* as the devil's apprentice declares, "We want cattle who can finally become food; He wants servants who can finally become sons."[15] Guite echoes the point when he continues:

Here is a joy that makes the spirit leap
And makes the humble greater than they
*   now   .   .   .*

---

[13] Guite, "Jupiter II" in *After Prayer*, 45.

[14] Guite, "Jupiter I" in *After Prayer*, 44.

[15] C.S. Lewis, *The Screwtape Letters* (New York: HarperOne, 2000) Letter 8, 39.

Rich music stirs your spirit, solemn, slow
Whose true nobility still draws you up
Beyond yourself with blessings to bestow.
Come, fill the cup.[16]

Courageous battle is yet required – that is the fun of *Halo* and *Destiny* -- which Guite illustrates in his *Mars*:

Rise up and stand for what you know is
*   right*
Marshall your strength and take the upper
*   hand . . .*
The red rose kindles to a flaming brand
When Love needs her defenders. Though
*   the night*
Is long and dark, deliverance is at hand!
So, battle-hardened, fearless in the fight,
Rise up and stand.[17]

By contrast, the efforts of marauding aggressors ring hollow with the call:

Rise up and stand to grasp with iron will
The spoils of war, the conquest of the land.
Whilst there is war to wage and blood to
spill

---

[16] Guite, "Jupiter I" in *After Prayer*, 44.

[17] Guite, "Mars I" in *After Prayer*, 42.

Rise up and stand.[18]

Such courage required of *Halo*'s noble Spartans and *Destiny*'s Guardians of Earth and humanity echoes throughout classical literature. J.R.R. Tolkien, creator of *The Hobbit* and *The Lord of the Rings*, found the model for such bravery in Norse mythology like *Beowulf*, as gods fought alongside heroes, the threat of extinction for all looming ominously:

> In Norse, at any rate, the gods are within Time, doomed with their allies to death. Their battle is with the monsters and the outer darkness. They gather heroes for the final defense . . . It is the strength of the northern mythological imagination that it faced this problem, put the monsters in the centre, gave them victory but no honour, and found a potent but terrible solution in naked will and courage. "As a working theory absolutely impregnable."[19]

Greek and Roman gods, by contrast, did not face such existential threat, and thus offered less

---

[18] Guite, "Mars II" in *After Prayer*, 43.

[19] J.R.R. Tolkien, "The Monsters and the Critics" in *The Monsters and the Critics and Other Essays* (London: HarperCollins, 2006), 25-26.

in the way of inspiration, Tolkien claimed: "So potent is it [northern mythology's central theme of courage], that while the older southern imagination has faded forever into literary ornament, the northern has power, as it were, to revive its spirit even in our own times."[20] But the Norse genius reflects an even longer tradition of cosmic struggle, that found in Scripture.

Tolkien claimed that *Beowulf*'s allusions to scripture were key in giving such Norse fables their spiritual power. War between giants and God himself, as well as references to Cain, show how "elements of Scripture" and the "noble pagan of old days," "new Scripture and old tradition," the "noble pagan of old days," "touched and ignited."[21] The themes are precisely the same, Tolkien claimed: "Man alien in a hostile world, engaged in a struggle which he cannot win while the world lasts . . . that his courage noble in itself is also the highest loyalty."[22]

---

[20] Tolkien, "The Monsters and the Critics" in *The Monsters and the Critics*, 26.

[21] Ibid.

[22] Ibid.

Guite's final and fifteenth poem of the sequence (there were two for each of the seven planets used), *Destiny: Earth's Enigmas*, reflects the greater spiritual backdrop to such heroics as those of *Halo*, *Destiny*, *Beowulf*, and Frodo Baggins, and is introduced as an embodiment of "Bungie's vision of 'Guardians,' 'The City,' 'The Darkness' & More."[23]

The poem, an "eightfold rhyme" (eight stanzas of eight lines each), speaks of the mysterious origins of *Destiny*'s world:

> *Riddles of the shadowed path . . .*
> *Set against dark and dread*
> *Cryptic clue and fragile thread*
> *Sent to those with eyes to see"*
> *Who may find in the*
> *Hidden patterns of the past*
> *Might reclaim what you have lost*
> *Secrets kept by saint and sage*

and consoles the combatants that:

---

[23] Malcolm Guite, *The Music of the Spheres: a poetic adventure resumes*, February 23, 2019, malcolmguite.wordpress.com/tag/destiny/.

All   your   hope   is   not   in   vain
Seven   heavens   over   earth
Bring that common hope to birth.[24]

Scriptural allusion can be found throughout the poem, for those "with eyes to see" (Matthew 13:16), also including statements like "night comes when no man can work" (John 9:4) and "our hope is not in vain" (1 Corinthians 15:14). Lines speaking of an unheard music directly refer to the poem's theme of the music of the spheres, in which may be found salvation, as noble (and gaming) warriors are implored to "seek within that hidden light / through whose music you unite."[25] T.S. Eliot's renowned poetry lends to the drama and the message, as Guite alludes to his 1922 poem *The Wasteland*, in which Eliot bemoaned the spiritual exhaustion of the post-World War I world, with:

In   the   darkness,   cold,   accurst
where   the   wasteland   does   its   worst

---

[24] Malcolm Guite, *Destiny: Earth's Enigma*, 2013, www.malcolmguite.wordpress.com/tag/destiny/.

[25] Guite, *Destiny*.

loyalty may fail and lapse every living truth collapse.[26]

Eliot's thought also appears in the idea that in the hidden music of the spheres can be found humanity's redemption. In his *Four Quartets*, structured after *The Wasteland* though written two decades later and after he had come to faith, Eliot encourages us to seek the hidden sounds, the laughter and the music, "Not known, because not looked for / But heard, half-heard, in the stillness."[27] Salvation for the Guardians consists in finding those who can answer the call:

Who can count the ages gone?
Who can hear the hidden song?
Who is he who feels and hears
Long-lost music of the spheres?
Hears the secret symphony
Sevenfold in harmony.[28]

---

[26] Guite, *Destiny.*

[27] T.S. Eliot, "Little GIdding V" in *The Complete Poems and Plays 1909 – 1950* (New York: Harcourt, 1971),145.

[28] Guite, *Destiny: Earth's Enigma.*

An earlier poem of Guite's is instructive here. In *The Singing Bowl*, we are instructed to not just seek but to reflect and become this hidden music:

Begin the song exactly where you are.
Remain within the world of which you're
    made.
Call nothing common in the earth or air . .
Become an open singing bowl, whose
    chime
Is richness rising out of emptiness,
And timelessness resounding into time.[29]

Eliot implored us likewise to listen for "the music heard so deeply / That it is not heard at all, but you are the music / while the music lasts."[30]

The strongest spiritual imagery of *Destiny: Earth's Enigmas* is that of the Traveler. Celestial hope for the Spartans of *Halo*, the Traveler is a dormant but protective orb hovering above The City of *Destiny*'s Guardians, and assumes the dimensions of Christ in the cryptic lines of *Destiny: Earth's Enigmas*. His otherworldly origins inform man's earliest beginnings,

---

[29] Malcolm Guite, "The Singing Bowl," in *The Singing Bowl: Collected poems by Malcolm Guite* (Norwich: Canterbury Press, 2013), xv.

[30] Eliot, *The Dry Salvages* V, 136.

seek the one who travels far
from the deepest roots long drawn

and provide a hopeful prelude:

to the city's golden dawn
quickened life begins to stir
a long awaited messenger.[31]

The two final stanzas paint a picture of a Traveler which is the hope of ages, as they begin:

Far above the city's domes
Seek the Traveler when he comes

Even in the blackest night
From the Darkness springs a Light

Which provides both our destiny and our purpose

Find the end where you begin
Light without and Light within
Seek the secret sages know
Light above and Light below.[32]

Guite's "the end where you begin" also famously appears in Eliot's *Four Quartets*, referencing the final words of Mary Queen of Scots as she faced execution, declaring that upon death

---

[31] Guite, *Destiny: Earth's Enigma.*

[32] Ibid.

her (eternal) life was just about to begin, "in my end is my beginning."[33] Eliot reverses them to claim that "in my beginning is my end" then encourages us to "not cease from exploration" as "the end of all our exploring / Will be to arrive where we started / And know the place for the first time."[34] [35] Once we (or any superhero) find our true beginning, just as Spartans and Guardians ensure their destiny by discovering the Traveler and the powerful rings which hail from earth's mysterious origins, then we will know our purpose, our end.

The Traveler's angelic, if not divine, significance is revealed in Guite's likening it to the Seraphim of the Old Testament, the highest of the angels, translated as "the burning ones," who appear in Isaiah's vision as six-winged creatures flying about the throne of God declaring "holy, holy, holy."[36] As Guite writes in the final stanza:

Seek in starlight soft and dim
Secrets of the seraphim

---

[33] Thomas Howard, *Dove Descending: A Journey into T.S. Eliot's Four Quartets* (San Francisco: Ignatius Press, 2006), loc. 806. Digital.

[34] Eliot, *East Coker* IV, 123.

[35] Eliot, *Little Gidding* V, 145.

[36] Isaiah 6:1-8.

Weapons no one else can wield
Patterned on a sacred shield
Where the spheres of heaven shine
Where the elements combine
Where the fearless and the free
Rise to meet their destiny.[37]

Just as the Traveler uses "weapons no one else can wield," so does Christ's atoning sacrifice on the cross defeat death itself with a weapon available only to him, the self-sacrifice of God Himself.

Final reflections on the pregnant spiritual significance that Guite's scribing lends to the *Halo* and *Destiny* stories can be found in reflecting on his Saturn poems. In Greek and Roman mythology, Saturn was associated with both suffering and the wisdom born of such suffering.[38] Guite's fallen Saturn poem bemoans senseless suffering:

In every heartbreak he is to be found
He is the end. He makes things fall apart.

---

[37] Guite, *Destiny: Earth's Enigma.*

[38] The Greek god Kronos, who became Saturn under the Romans, feared being overthrown by his children (as foretold in a prophecy) just as he had done to his own father Uranus, so he would eat his children upon their birth, until his wife Rhea gave him a swaddling stone in place of their sixth child Zeus, who later overthrew Saturn.

*There is a prison where his slaves are
bound* ...
He crushes hope before we even start ...
*In him there is no mercy to be found,
No truth, no grace, no beauty and no art,
Only the grave, the cold and stony ground*
In every heart.[39]

By contrast, suffering informed by, or leading to, knowledge of the deep mysteries, is the path to salvation, shown in Guite's poem of the redeemed Saturn:

*In every heart-break wisdom can be
    found,
The end of things may be the place to
    start* . . .
*We listen for the music; not a sound.
But we discover, silent and apart* . . .
*There is a deeper dance, an inner art
There is a hidden treasure to be found
In every heart.*[40]

That such suffering is unavoidable, the cost of the courageous battle with which it must often be met, is likewise affirmed by Eliot's poem. "Not fare well, but fare forward, voyagers," Eliot inveighs,

---

[39] Guite, "Saturn II" in *After Prayer*, 47.

[40] Guite, "Saturn I" in *After Prayer*, 46.

referring to Krishna's advice to Arjuna (Indian mythical superheroes) on the battlefield in which he granted blessings to combatants on both sides: the moral struggle will continue.[41] This suffering, borne with courage and finding in silence the music half-heard which is the true music of the spheres, enables the brave soul, like the Spartans of *Halo* and the Guardians of *Destiny*, and implores us, as in Guite's *Destiny* poem, to:

> *Find the end where you begin*
> *Light without and Light within*
> *seek the secret sages know*
> *Light above and Light below.*[42]

Guite and *Halo/Destiny* follow Eliot further here, who yet held out hope, citing the medieval Christian mystic Julian of Norwich, that "all *shall* be well, and all manner of thing shall be well" once this light is found.[43] More significantly, most significantly, they affirm the wisdom of Ecclesiastes (3:11) from long ago, that "He has placed eternity in our hearts," and we -- or any

---

[41] Eliot, *The Four Quartets: The Dry Salvages* III, 135.

[42] Guite, *Destiny: Earth's Enigma.*

[43] Eliot, *Little Gidding* V, 145.

Superhero -- need only listen to find it, and follow it with courage.

Resources

To Connect with An Unexpected Journal

An Unexpected Journal is published quarterly; however, the conversation does not end. Join us on social media for discussion with the authors weekly:

An Unexpected Journal online:
http://anunexpectedjournal.com

On Facebook:
https://www.facebook.com/anunexpectedjournal/

On Twitter: https://twitter.com/anujournal

On Instagram:
https://www.instagram.com/anujournal/

On Pinterest:
https://www.pinterest.com/anunexpectedjournal/

Comments and feedback can be submitted at
http://anunexpectedjournal.com/contact/

Be sure to sign up for our newsletter for announcements on new editions and events near you:
http://anunexpectedjournal.com/newsletter

TO READ MORE

When discussing theology, or philosophy, or literature, or art, one is stepping into and taking part of a larger conversation that has been taking place for centuries. Each essay within the journal contains not only the thoughts of the individual author, but draws upon works and thinkers of the past. It is our hope that the writing not only engages your interest in the specific essay topic, but that you join us in the Great Conversation.

To read more, please visit http://anunexpectedjournal.com/resources/ for a list of the works cited within the essays of the journal.

SUBSCRIBE

Yearly subscriptions to *An Unexpected Journal* are available through our web site. Please visit http://anunexpectedjournal.com/subscribe for more information. For bulk pricing, events, or speaking requests, please send an email to anunexpectedjournal@gmail.com.

About An Unexpected Journal

The Inspiration

J.R.R. Tolkien and C.S. Lewis, both members of The Inklings writers group, are well-known for their fiction embedded with Christian themes. These fantasy writers, who were also philosophers and teachers, understood the important role imagination plays in both exercising and expanding the faculties of the mind as well as the development of faith.

Beyond the parables of Jesus, their works are the gold standard for imaginative apologetics. The title, *An Unexpected Journal*, is a nod to the work to which Tolkien devoted much of his life, *The Lord of the Rings*.

Our Story

An Unexpected Journal is the endeavor of a merry band of Houston Baptist University Master of Arts in Apologetics students and alumni. What began as simply a Facebook post on November 1, 2017 wishing that there was an outlet for imaginative apologetics quickly organized by the end of the year into a very real and very exciting quarterly publication.

Our Mission

An Unexpected Journal seeks to demonstrate the truth of Christianity through both reason and the imagination to engage the culture from a Christian worldview.

OUR CONTRIBUTORS

James W. Baker

Jesse W. Baker is a United Methodist pastor in North Carolina. He holds a Master of Divinity from Duke Divinity School and is (much too slowly) taking classes at Houston Baptist University, pursuing a Master of Arts in Apologetics (cultural track). Traveling with family, reading C.S. Lewis, preaching, and teaching are among his greatest joys in life.

Donald W. Catchings, Jr.
www.donaldwcatchingsjr.com

Donald W. Catchings, Jr. is Founder and Board Chair of Street Light Inc. and Pastor of The True Light Church in Conroe, Texas since 2009. Donald regularly contributes to *An Unexpected Journal* and has published various titles including his most recent release, *Strength in Weakness* — a Young Adult reimagining of the Theseus Myth.

Annie Crawford
www.anniecrawford.net

Annie Crawford lives in Austin, Texas with her husband and three teenage daughters. She currently homeschools, teaches humanities courses, and serves on the Faith & Culture team at Christ Church Anglican while working to complete a Masters of Apologetics at Houston Baptist University.

Joseph Holmes

www.theoverthinkersjournal.com

Joseph Holmes is an award-nominated filmmaker and culture critic living in New York City whose words have been published in The New York Times, Forbes, and Religion Unplugged. He is co-host of the podcast The Overthinkers and its companion website theoverthinkersjournal.com where he discusses art, culture, faith and art with his fellow overthinkers.

Christy Luis

www.linktr.ee/christaaay

Christy Luis has worked as a library assistant and currently runs a YouTube channel called "Dostoevsky in Space," where she talks about books and organizes public reading events. She has an Associate of Arts in Humanities and graduated cum laude from Regent University with a Bachelor of Arts in English from Regent University.

Jason Monroe

Jason holds a B.A. from York College in York, NE, where he studied English and Psychology. He also recently completed his M.A. in Christian Apologetics from Houston Baptist University. Along with research and writing, Jason plays drums in a band and works in the mental health field. He grew up in Pierre, SD and currently lives in Spearfish, SD. In his spare time does a lot of outdoors activities in the Black Hills area and volunteers at his local parish."

Seth Myers
www.narnianfrodo.com

Seth Myers completed his MA in Cultural Apologetics from Houston Baptist University in 2017. As a power systems engineer, he has been involved with transformer diagnostics and rural electrification projects by partnering with NGOs in West Africa. A volunteer with international students through local churches, he enjoys conversations with friends from all cultures. He considers himself rich in friendships across time and space, including but not limited to C.S. Lewis, J.R.R. Tolkien, Bede the Venerable, Augustine, Ravi Zacharias & friends, and many student friends (chess-playing when possible, but not required) typically from throughout Asia. He has recently begun taking online courses in Faulkner University's Doctor of Humanities program.

Annie Nardone
www.AnnieNardone.com

Annie Nardone is a two-year C.S. Lewis Institute Fellow with a Master of Arts degree in Cultural Apologetics from Houston Baptist University. She has homeschooled her three kids for twenty-five years and taught art and humanities at her local co-op. Her heart is for Rohan, Narnia, and Hogwarts, far fairer lands than this. Annie contributes and edits for *An Unexpected Journal* at www.anunexpectedjournal.com. She publishes online at www.literarylife.org, www.theperennialgen.com, and most recently began writing for the online magazine *Cultivating* at www.thecultivatingproject.com. She also wrote an historical cookbook for Bright Ideas Press. She can be contacted at: the.annie.nardone@gmail.com.

Cherish Nelson
Cherish Nelson is an adjunct professor of World Religions at Kankakee Community College

and the Director of Youth Ministries at Kankakee Asbury United Methodist Church. She has a B.A. in English from Olivet Nazarene University and a M.A. in Apologetics from Houston Baptist University, where she specialized in Cultural Apologetics. Cherish also creates and shares apologetics curriculum for youth groups. Her apologetic interests include the historicity of the resurrection, the problem of evil, and imaginative apologetics.

Cherish has a long-standing passion for building a confident faith in her students. She integrates Christian education and discipleship into the retreats, mission trips, and outreach events she organizes. Cherish is particularly interested in integrating the arts into youth ministry to supplement traditional propositional teaching. Throughout her time in ministry and academia, Cherish has written apologetics curriculum for youth groups related to fiction and poetry, science and faith, the resurrection, and the problem of evil.

Megan Joy Rials

Megan Joy Rials holds her Juris Doctor and Graduate Diploma in Comparative Law from the

Louisiana State University Paul M. Hebert Law Center and works as a research attorney in Baton Rouge, Louisiana. She is currently working toward an online Master of Arts in Apologetics (cultural track) from Houston Baptist University. Her work has previously been published in An Unexpected Journal and the Louisiana Law Review, where she served as Production Editor for Volume 77. She attends Jefferson Baptist Church with her family, and her main apologetics interests lie in storytelling of all mediums, fantasy literature, and the work of the Inklings, particularly C. S. Lewis and Dorothy Sayers.

Jason M. Smith
www.jackwootton.com

Jason Smith serves on the board of An Unexpected Journal and as senior editor for acquisitions and development at Wootton Major Publishing. In his spare time, he works a day job as a technical writer and marketing strategist for a medical device engineering firm, where he writes about fun things like FDA regulations and embedded cybersecurity. He is the pseudonymous author of the much-loved young adult fantasy series Fayborn and reviews every book he reads at www.goodreads.com/mrwootton.

James M. Swayze
www.adcaelos.com

An apologist and writer, as well as a father of four, Jim lives in Dallas, Texas with his wife, Cristi, two golden retrievers, and two formerly-feral cats. He read Philosophy and English as an undergrad at SMU and obtained a graduate degree in Apologetics from Houston Baptist University. A frequent blogger, Jim travels the United States giving lectures on all things related to C.S. Lewis. For the past few years he has led a popular reading and discussion group called "The Inklings." In his spare time, he likes to fly fish and drink Oregon Pinot noir (though not at the same time).

John P. Tuttle

John Tuttle is a Catholic journalist and creative. He has written for The Hill, University Bookman, Eucatastrophe, CiRCE Institute, Franciscan Media, Starting Points Journal, The Millions, and the University of Notre Dame's Grotto Network. He also contributed a chapter to the book The Right to Believe (Vide Press 2020).

Tuttle has previously served as the prose editor of Loomings, the literary magazine of Benedictine College.

Clark Weidner
www.thesolidfaith.com

Clark Weidner is the founder of Solid Faith: A Podcast, blog, vlog, and Christian apologetics medium. He is holds a Masters degree in Cultural Apologetics from Houston Baptist University. He has a blue belt in jiu jitsu and plenty of scars from years of skateboarding. He met his wife Amber in a Lord of the Rings book club and now they have a dog named Thanos (due to their love of comics).

Thoughts from a Fellow Traveler

By Jack Tollers

If you aren't a Christian and have somehow gotten to the point where you are reading this, then I must warn you about the pebble in your shoe. For that is what it is like to be around Christians who discuss things together, whether or not they are "Christian kinds of things" that are discussed. At a certain point you will notice something about their point of view, something in their underlying assumptions, and to be honest when you do it will become quite annoying.

That is the pebble I was referring to.

But it gets worse.

Maybe it is not your fault that you happen to be reading this, and you've done a pretty good job milling about life without bumping into too much of this sort of Christian stuff. It could be the case that you haven't really made a conscious effort to avoid Christianity, but chances are (if you are reading this) that is going to change. Somewhere along the line, perhaps even in the course of reading this journal, even, a pebble has worked its way into your shoe, and eventually the pebble will have to be dealt with.

It's not my job to tell you what it is. (I don't really know what "it" is in your case. All I know is that when the pebble got into my shoe, it got to the point where I couldn't walk much further without annoying my heel something terrible.) What I can do is suggest to you something that would have helped me if I had come across it in the back of some obscure journal: The pebble does not exist for itself. The pebble makes you stop and deal with the pebble. Stopping to deal with the pebble leads to thinking about your shoe. Then you start thinking about how much further up the trail you'd be if it weren't for that blasted pebble, which leads to thoughts about the trail itself and the path you're walking . . . and so on.

A particular Christian, or a particular thought expressed by a Christian, or perhaps just the particular quality you meet in places and things of

Christian origin will eventually function to put you in mind of something beyond or behind themselves. I say something because I'm trying to be non-partisan, but really I mean someone. Because at some point, the context for these thoughts will change to an awareness that this Christ person has been behind all of it.

When this moment comes, avoid mistaking Jesus for the pebble in your shoe. (If you do, it won't be long before another pebble gets in there and starts the whole thing off again. It took me years to figure that out.) Instead, consider the possibility that he is more like the path than the pebble. He said as much himself when he told Thomas, "I am the way, the truth and the life. No man comes to the Father except by me."

The truth aspect of Jesus' claim is, of course, exclusive. But there is more to his self disclosure. The other terms, "the way" and "the life" point us beyond a mere static assertion of fact or a single point of view toward a dynamic process of relational involvement. The pursuit of truth leads to knowing Jesus (if he indeed is truth incarnate). Thus, just as travelers come to know a country by living in it and exploring it, so people will grow in their knowledge of Truth as they make their way through life, the path itself bringing us in proximity to Jesus.

Such a journey, so conceived, is bound to take a person through some interesting experiences, and to unexpected places. Once the pebble is out of the shoe.

All the way to heaven is heaven for he said, "I am the way" — St. Catherine of Sienna

"And ye shall seek me, and find me, when ye shall search for me with all your heart." — Jeremiah 29:13

An Unexpected Journal

The Abolition of Man

Spring 2018   Volume 1, Issue 1

Subscribe to our newsletter at

www.anunexpectedjournal.com/subscribe

and receive a **free digital edition** of our first issue!

AUJ Issues

If you enjoy discussing faith, apologetics, and culture, don't miss an issue of *An Unexpected Journal*. Find this issues at your online bookstores, digital book sellers, or request your library to carry the journal.

For bulk, corporate, or ministry orders, please contact the journal at anunexpectedjournal@gmail.com

Yearly subscriptions and sets may be purchased at http://anunexpectedjournal.com/subscribe/

Volume 1 (2018)

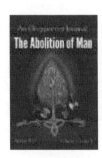   

Spring: The Abolition of Man

Summer: The Power of Story

Fall: Courage, Strength & Hope

Advent: Planet Narnia

Volume 2 (2019)

Spring:	**Summer:**	**Fall:**	**Advent:**
Imagination	Film & Music	Dystopia	G.K. Chesterton

Volume 3 (2020)

Spring:	**Summer:**	**Fall:**	**Advent:**
The Worlds of Tolkien	Science Fiction	Medieval Minds	George MacDonald

Volume 4 (2021)

Fall:
The
Ancients

Advent:
Ordway's
Imaginative
Harvest

Spring:
Image
Bearers

Summer:
Superheroes

Made in the USA
Columbia, SC
24 June 2021